CAMBRIDGE LIBRARY COLLECTION

Books of enduring scholarly value

History of Oceania

This series focuses on Australia, New Zealand and the Pacific region from the arrival of European seafarers and missionaries to the early twentieth century. Contemporary accounts document the gradual development of the European settlements from penal colonies and whaling stations to thriving communities of farmers, miners and traders with fully-fledged administrative and legal systems. Particularly noteworthy are the descriptions of the indigenous peoples of the various islands, their customs, and their differing interactions with the European settlers.

The Mines of South Australia

The British journalist and mining expert John Baptist Austin (1827–96) moved to Adelaide as a young man with his family. During the 1850s he became closely involved in the South Australian mining industry and the gold rush in Victoria. Austin was rewarded for his outstanding expertise and became secretary of several corporations, including the Adelaide and West Kanmantoo mining companies. His extensive knowledge is reflected in this work, first published in 1863. Offering a first-hand account of South Australian mining culture, it contains a great many descriptions of individual mines along with details of the everyday life of the miners. The book also provides insight into the region's Cornish mining heritage: many mines were named 'Wheal', family names such as 'Rodda' are mentioned, and direct comparisons of the mineralogy and the regulations for mineral prospecting are made.

Cambridge University Press has long been a pioneer in the reissuing of out-of-print titles from its own backlist, producing digital reprints of books that are still sought after by scholars and students but could not be reprinted economically using traditional technology. The Cambridge Library Collection extends this activity to a wider range of books which are still of importance to researchers and professionals, either for the source material they contain, or as landmarks in the history of their academic discipline.

Drawing from the world-renowned collections in the Cambridge University Library and other partner libraries, and guided by the advice of experts in each subject area, Cambridge University Press is using state-of-the-art scanning machines in its own Printing House to capture the content of each book selected for inclusion. The files are processed to give a consistently clear, crisp image, and the books finished to the high quality standard for which the Press is recognised around the world. The latest print-on-demand technology ensures that the books will remain available indefinitely, and that orders for single or multiple copies can quickly be supplied.

The Cambridge Library Collection brings back to life books of enduring scholarly value (including out-of-copyright works originally issued by other publishers) across a wide range of disciplines in the humanities and social sciences and in science and technology.

The Mines
of South Australia
Including Also an Account
of the Smelting Works
in that Colony

J.B. AUSTIN

CAMBRIDGE
UNIVERSITY PRESS

CAMBRIDGE UNIVERSITY PRESS

Cambridge, New York, Melbourne, Madrid, Cape Town,
Singapore, São Paolo, Delhi, Mexico City

Published in the United States of America by Cambridge University Press, New York

www.cambridge.org
Information on this title: www.cambridge.org/9781108057615

© in this compilation Cambridge University Press 2013

This edition first published 1863
This digitally printed version 2013

ISBN 978-1-108-05761-5 Paperback

THE

MINES OF SOUTH AUSTRALIA,

INCLUDING ALSO AN ACCOUNT OF THE

𝕾melting 𝕸orks in that 𝕮olony;

TOGETHER WITH

A BRIEF DESCRIPTION OF THE COUNTRY,

AND

INCIDENTS OF TRAVEL IN THE BUSH.

ILLUSTRATED BY A MAP.

By J. B. AUSTIN.

ADELAIDE:

C. PLATTS, E. S. WIGG, G. DEHANE, J. HOWELL, W. C. RIGBY,
G. MULLETT, AND ALL BOOKSELLERS.

MELBOURNE, PARIS, AND NEW YORK: F. F. BAILLIERE, PUBLISHER IN ORDINARY
TO THE VICTORIAN GOVERNMENT.

SYDNEY: A. CUBITT, AND G. SANDS.   TASMANIA: WALCH & SONS.

LONDON: LONGMAN & CO., PATERNOSTER-ROW.

AND ALL BOOKSELLERS.

MDCCCLXIII.

First Edition of Three Thousand.]

PRINTED AT THE ADVERTISER AND CHRONICLE OFFICES, ADELAIDE.

DEDICATION

TO HIS EXCELLENCY SIR DOMINICK DALY,

Knight, Governor-in-Chief of the Province of South Australia, and Vice-Admiral of the same.

SIR,

The high position which you occupy in this Province naturally suggests the desirability of dedicating to your Excellency a work on the Mines of the Colony; but independently of your official position, another reason is found in the warm interest shown by your Excellency in everything pertaining to the welfare of South Australia.

It is a happy circumstance for the Colony to be blest with a Governor who can appreciate the importance of the objects of the present little work; and it affords me, therefore, the sincerest pleasure to inscribe it to your Excellency, for this reason, as well as from motives of the highest personal esteem.

I have the honor to be

Your Excellency's

Obliged and obedient servant,

J. B. AUSTIN.

LIST OF SUBSCRIBERS.

His Excellency Sir D. Daly, Governor-in-Chief
His Honor the Chief Justice
The Hon. the Chief Secretary (G. M. Waterhouse)
The Hon. the Attorney-General (R. I. Stow)
The Hon. the Treasurer (A. Blyth)
The Hon. the Commissioner of Crown Lands (H. B. T. Strangways)
The Hon. the Commissioner of Public Works (W. Milne)
The Hon. the President of the Legislative Council (Sir J. H. Fisher)
The Hon. the Speaker of the House of Assembly (G. C. Hawker)
The Hon. G. F. Angas
The Hon. G. Hall
The Hon. G. Tinline
The Hon. S. Davenport
The South Australian Company
Thomas Elder, Esq.
The Moonta Mining Company
The Wallaroo Mining Company
Henry Martin, Esq. (Superintendent, Yudanamutana Mining Company)
Karkarilla Mining Company
Talisker Mining Company
Yelta Mining Company
Kirwan Mining Company
South Australian Mining Association (Burra)
Kanyaka Mining Company
Charles Bonney, Esq. (Manager, Great Northern Mining Company)
Napoleon Mining Company
New Cornwall Mining Company
North Rhine Mining Company
Wirrawilka Mining Company
The Patent Copper Company
Captain P. Morrison (Great Northern Mines)
Captain H. R. Hancock
Captain J. B. Pascoe
South Australian Banking Company
National Bank of Australasia
Bank of Australasia
Messrs. A. L. Elder (London)
  " Alexander Scrutton (Stock Exchange, London)
  " T. A. Austin (Ditto.)
  " A. H. Gouge

Messrs. J. Stilling & Co.
  " F. H. Faulding & Co.
  " H. C. Gleeson
  " Alfred Frost
  " A. P. Burtt
  " H. Alford
  " Wright Brothers
  " John Baker
  " Levi & Co.
  " Samuel Court, Money Order Office, London
  " Wm. Sheffield, Solicitor, London
  " J. T. Bagot, M.P.
  " Neville Blyth, M.P.
  " T. Magarey, M.P.
  " John Colton, M.P.
  " W. Bakewell, M.P.
  " H. Mildred, M.P.
  " John Hart, M.P.
  " J. B. Neales, M.P.
  " R. R. Torrens (Registrar-General)
  " E. M. Bagot
  " J. Hodgkiss
  " H. Noltenius
  " G. Wyatt
  " Edmund Bowman
  " S. Stocks
  " Henry T. Morris
  " W. Fowler
  " E. M. Martin
  " W. Bartley
  " C. Smedley
  " John Western
  " G. Boothby
Dr. Mayo
Dr. Gosse
Dr. Bayer
Dr. Whittell
Dr. Wheeler
Dr. Todman
Dr. Taylor
Rev. Julian Edmund Woods, F.G.S., and F.R.S., Victoria
Rev. F. W. Cox
Rev. A. R. Russell
The Very Rev. Dean Farrell
Rev. C. Manthorpe
Rev. J. Watsford
Rev. C. Farr, M.A., St. Peter's College
Rev. James Lyall
Rev. John Gardner
Rev. George Stonehouse

Rev. Robt. Haining
Rev. C. W. Evan
Rev. W. Harcus
Rev. John Smythe, (R. C. C.)
Messrs. R. Stuckey
" D. Culley
" F. J. Beck & Co.
" W. B. Dawes
" David Randall
" G. Muller
" T. Schumacher
" S. Pearce
" R. S. Crabb
" N. V. Squarey
" Goode & Cussen
" J. & A. Hallett
" E. J. Peake, S. M.
" W. Gawen
" G. & H. Bartleet
" R. Hall
" C. G. Everard
" S. Duryea
" Green, Parr, & Luxmore
" Joseph Gilbert
" Johnston, Furniss, & Blakeway
" W. J. Brown
" J. T. Fitch
" W. Finke
" J. L. Young
" W. Younghusband, Jun., & Co.
" G. & R. Wills & Co.
" Skelton & Co.
" Acraman, Main, Lindsay, & Co.
" H. C. Palmer
" —— Causby
" J. B. Hughes
" W. Main
" C. D'Oyley Cooper
" E. McEllister
" W. W. Tuxford
" Lyshon Jones (Superintendent
    Smelting Works, Wallaroo)
" J. D. Woods

Messrs. C. S. Hare
" Green & Wadham
" Townsend Duryea
" Bull & Whitington
" J. Darwent
" J. Perryman
" Townsend, Botting, & Kay
" Arthur Hardy
" W. Goddard
" W. Hitchcox
" John Chambers
" Giles & Smith
" Richard Hicks
" Andrews & Bonin
" S. J. Way
" E. K. Horn
" Joel Lyons
" St. George & Smythe
" Stephen King
" W. Butterworth, Yankalilla
" Thomas Wilson
" G. W. Hawkes, S.M.
" Fredk. G. Waterhouse
" Adolph Gaedechens
" Charles Fenn
The Consul for France
    "   Denmark
    "   Hamburg
    "   Bremen
    "   Portugal
    "   America
    "   Belgium
    "   Chili
The Hon. G. Rolfe, Melbourne
G. M. Larnach, Esq., Melbourne
M. W. Taylor, Esq., Melbourne
William Noall, Esq., Melbourne
James Edward Neild, Esq., Melbourne
Henry Sheffield, Esq., Public Library,
    Melbourne
Dr. Embling, Melbourne
F. Mueller, M.D., F.B.S., Melbourne

[Total number of Copies subscribed for, 1,200]

PREFACE.

THE growing importance of the Mining Interest in this Colony, and the evident want of general and correct information respecting our Mineral resources, suggested to me the idea of making a tour of all the Mines, and publishing the result of my observations. The book, although not professing to be a scientific work, may prove, in an humble degree, a not inappropriate sequel to a very valuable work on the Geology of the Colony, by the Rev. Julian Edmund Woods, F.G.S., and F.R.S. (Victoria).

To guard against the possibility of loss, I drew up a Prospectus soliciting subscriptions to the work; and I feel great satisfaction in referring to the List of Subscribers, as a proof of the confidence placed in me, and also of the great importance attached to the Mining Interest of the Colony.

About four months were occupied in visiting the Mines and collecting information, and during this time I travelled about 1,800 miles, chiefly on horseback.

I hope this work will be found especially interesting and important to readers in England, and elsewhere, who may desire information respecting our Mines, and which is not at present to be found in any other book. It is, I believe, 17 years since any detailed account of the Mines of this Colony was published in a collective form, and this was in a valuable work by F. S. Dutton, Esq., and entitled "South Australia and its Mines." At that time the Copper Mines enumerated were eight, and the Lead Mines three in number! I trust so long an interval will not elapse before an enlarged edition of the present work will be required.

I have to express my obligations to those numerous friends who have assisted me in various ways; to the settlers in the North who aided me with horses, and whose genuine hospitality cheered and refreshed me on my toilsome journey; to the members of the Government, who rendered me all the information I required; and though last, not least, to those who have subscribed so liberally to the work. I trust it will not disappoint their expectations.

J. B. AUSTIN.

Adelaide, March, 1863.

INTRODUCTORY.

Having for some years taken a great interest in Mineralogy, and having paid especial attention to mining matters during my recent connection with the Adelaide press, the idea suggested itself to me that a work on the Mines of South Australia would, at the present time, prove not merely interesting but useful. It is well known in this country and elsewhere that a mining mania has, for above two years past, held possession of the community, and from the commencement of mineral discovery in the colony, no fewer than 1,720 mining "claims" have been applied for to the 31st Dec., 1862; 1,576 of them during the last three years. The large majority of these represent 80 acres of land to each claim, and where the claim is "taken up" a rent of 10s. per acre is paid to the Government under the present regulations. The leases are for 14 years, renewable at the end of the term on payment of a fine. It will be seen that a very large amount of capital, considering the smallness of our community, is invested every year in mining. But although so many claims have been applied for, the number of Mines actually being worked is very small in proportion. It must be explained that every claim does not represent a separate lode or discovery of mineral, nor does it necessarily indicate the existence of mineral at all; for, with that spirit of speculation apparently so inseparable from mining, as soon as a good discovery is made by one party there is frequently a rush to the Land Office, and others take out claims all round, merely with the hope of finding something, and often without any knowledge of the locality on the part of the speculators.

I have thought these few words of explanation necessary for the benefit of readers not acquainted with the colony; and before proceeding with the subject under consideration, I would add a few remarks respecting the mode in which I determined to deal with it. Before starting on my journey I was strongly urged to visit *every mineral claim*, and if I had had time and means at my command I should have been glad to have done so; but it was no part of my original design to visit claims on which no work had been done, but to describe only the *Mines* of the colony,—no matter how small, so long as they were entitled to the name. However, I have visited as many claims as I was able to see, and I may state that with reference to many of them I have come to the conclusion that it would be unfair to the proprietors and also to the public, for me to express an opinion respecting them in a work like the present. I refer more particularly to claims which are strictly private property, not being offered for sale, nor being worked by a public company.

In writing the following pages I have kept in view the fact that the book is likely to fall into the hands of English readers, and of many others unacquainted with the interior of this colony ; and I have considered that the introduction of a description of our mode of travelling and of bush life would relieve the dullness almost inseparable from a mere dry detail of shafts and drives, lodes and cross-courses. I have aimed rather at giving an intelligible and popular description of the Mines, than at writing in too technical language.

Perhaps this chapter would be the most fitting place for expressing my views as to the usual plan of disposing of mineral properties. Whenever a discovery of Copper Ore—I might almost say of Copper *stains*—is made, it is held, by interested persons, as entitled to be called "a mine." It is not difficult to find a man bearing the title of " Captain"—perhaps assumed, perhaps entirely honorary—to write a glowing report of this " wonderful discovery ; which must pay its working expenses at least, from the very first day that a pick is struck into the ground, and will, in all probability, pay handsome dividends to the fortunate proprietors in an incredibly short time."

The experience of mining, during the last seventeen years, in this colony, does not warrant the confident assurance, that even rich surface indications will result in the development of a valuable mine ; and my opinion is, that the fairest plan to pursue in dealing with a mineral property intended to be sold, would be to sink one or two shafts, or cross-cuts, according to the nature of the country, to a sufficient depth to prove at least that there was a Copper-bearing lode *going down* a few fathoms, before asking a high price for it. I have seen many "mineral claims" which the owners tried to persuade me were some of "the finest mines in the country," but on which not a day's work had been done, and where, in my opinion, there was nothing to indicate that any Ore-bearing lode would be found below the surface. It is very true there might be a few pretty specimens of green and blue carbonates, or even grey and red oxides, on the surface, but as I have before said, it does not follow that these Ores will continue to be found in depth ; as some of these surface deposits appear to have been made by the action of water. At the same time, there are many mineral sections, the value of which may be judged of with a great degree of certainty from the surface. Where, for instance, as is sometimes the case, a regular and well defined Copper-bearing lode, in favorable country, can be traced for a long distance, and, as often happens, the back of the lode is sufficiently exposed to show the walls and the underlay ; then we are warranted in supposing that we may meet with favorable results. On the other hand, it cannot be denied that some mines which presented every appearance of permanence, and yielded a fair quantity of good ore for some fathoms in depth, have apparently run out, and have in consequence been abandoned. In many, perhaps in most such cases, the abandonment has resulted from want of sufficient capital to prosecute the search ; as I am well aware there are many of our abandoned Mines which would be considered very promising properties in Cornwall.

To revert to the question of the disposal of mineral properties. Owing to the want of liberality in the mineral regulations of the colony it frequently happens that a poor man (comparatively speaking) who may have a good claim, has not the means of proving it; in such cases there can be no doubt that the fairest mode of procedure, instead of selling an unproved mine for a large sum, would be to raise a capital sufficient to develop it, and there is little difficulty in the way of such a course if the property promise to be a really good one. I consider the prices often put upon the mineral claims—mineral *leases* as they are in fact—are often fictitious ; for who can say until a Mine is developed, at least to some small extent, whether it is worth £20,000, or £10,000, or even £5,000. On this ground I conceive that it would be best for all parties that some amount of work should be done to prove a Mine before it is sold ; for a Mine worth £20,000 might be sold for £5,000 for want of a knowledge of its real value, or the reverse might happen with equal probability. I feel the importance of these remarks, because several instances have occurred in which " Mines" have been sold for a high price and turned out nearly valueless, whereas if proper precautions were taken, or some judicious system adopted with reference to the examination of mines by a competent party, before the purchase was completed, such unsatisfactory results would not be likely to occur. There is no doubt that in some cases it would have answered the purpose of English capitalists to have sent out a qualified person from England expressly to report on the property offered for sale ; not but that there are men in the colony of sufficient probity and understanding in such matters to qualify them to protect the interests of absentees ; but I mean to say that money would have been saved in the end by the expenditure at first of £200 or £300 in the way I have indicated.

We have lately had brought very prominently before the public in this colony, "The New Burra Burra Mining Company," a scheme which has been denounced by the leading journals of Adelaide as "a rank swindle." I confess when I read the prospectus and the accompanying "reports" I thought the exaggerations so palpable, that it was a matter of surprise how any one could have been deceived by them. The idea of courses of Ore 70 yards wide is something so very extraordinary, not to say unlikely, that it is astonishing that persons of any sense were so easily duped into believing the statement; and especially when nothing was known of the Mine in the colony, except by a favored few—Messrs. *Cave & Co.*, and who Messrs. Cave & Co. are does not very clearly appear. Mr. Cave is said to be a young man who was shepherding or stock-keeping for the Messrs. Chambers, and the *Co.* is *supposed* to be Mr. G. Francis, of Gawler, a man of rather higher attainments in geological knowledge than his partner. Mr. Francis has lately written to the public papers here, since the bubble has been exposed, repudiating the course pursued in reference to this Mine in England. I must confess that prior to my departure on my tour through the Northern Mines, I had heard nothing of the "New Burra Burra ;" it is true I had provided myself with a list of mineral claims from the Land Office, and in that list there were three applications in the name of Cave, the claims being held "*under right of search*." When I arrived in the far North, I was asked on two or three occasions if I had seen the Mine, and on my replying in the negative, and stating at the same time my intention to visit it, I was invariably met with a laugh, and was told that I might spare myself the trouble, for there was nothing to be seen. Subsequent enquiries resulted in the receipt of similar replies. Nevertheless, I made up my mind to go and judge for myself, but when I was actually on the road to the place, unavoidable circumstances prevented me from accomplishing my design, and I found I must either give up seeing the "New Burra Burra," or neglect other Mines which appeared to be of more importance. When I returned to Adelaide and saw the prospectus of the Mine in the English *Mining Journal*, I regretted that 1 had not remained a week or so longer in the North, and retraced my steps in order to visit it.

Some correspondence has taken place in the Adelaide papers respecting this Mine, and, as I said before, Mr. G. Francis wrote a letter repudiating the course pursued in England. In one of this gentleman's letters he expressed his willingness to accompany any person to the Mine who was qualified to judge on mining matters, alledging that although the Mine had been unwarrantably "puffed" in England there was a quantity of good Ore on the claims. I then wrote to Mr. Francis, agreeing to accept his offer, and was at the time prepared to start at once, but I received no reply to my letter, and I must now postpone my visit for some few months.

The Kapunda Mine.

IN a work like the present there is some slight difficulty in determining the order in which to notice the various mines. The proprietors of mines in one locality are jealous of those in another. The Wallaroo people affect an amount of disbelief in the Northern Mines, and those interested in the North, on the other hand, believe their Mines to be superior to those at Wallaroo. I had thought of noticing the Mines in the order of their discovery, but this plan would have been attended with some inconvenience, and I therefore decided on describing them as nearly as possible in reference to their geographical position. This will obviate certain little difficulties, and will enable me the more readily to introduce a description of the country traversed in visiting the Mines.

Starting from Adelaide in a northerly direction, we ride for 26 miles over plains between ranges of hills on the East, and the sea on the West, and varying in width from 8 to 12 miles. These plains, which at the time of the discovery of the Kapunda Mine were almost entirely uncultivated and occupied only as sheep runs, are now covered with farms, every available portion of them being either brought into cultivation or enclosed as grazing paddocks. After passing Gawler on the road to Kapunda the country becomes more hilly, and lightly timbered. There is nothing remarkable in the geological formation of the country until we reach the Kapunda Mine, after a ride of 24 miles from Gawler. This Mine is the oldest Copper Mine in the colony, having been discovered in 1843 by Mr. Francis S. Dutton and Mr. Charles Samuel Bagot (now of London), the youngest son of Capt. Charles Harvey Bagot, then a sheepfarmer and also a member of the Legislative Council. The Mine workings are on hilly ground of moderate elevation, and which was originally lightly timbered with peppermint gum, but the settlement of the adjoining township, the working of the mine, and above all the carrying on of smelting operations, have denuded the country of almost every stick of timber for miles round. Abundance, however, remains for the requirements of the Mine for some years to come, and within a moderate distance for cartage.

The first Ore was raised at the Kapunda Mine on the 8th January, 1844, and on the 23rd of the same month, five dray loads were dispatched to Adelaide. I had then just arrived in the colony, and well remember the excitement caused by this commencement of the development of one of the most important sources of the wealth of the colony. The Ore was good, the Mine promised well, and search soon began to be made for Copper Ore in other directions, and it was not long before further discoveries were announced.

With reference to the statistics of the Kapunda Mine I cannot do better than copy the following account from that concise and valuable little work, by my friend, Mr. Frederick Sinnett, " An Account of the Colony of South Australia, prepared for distribution at the International Exhibition of 1862 :"—

" On 4th March, 1845, the first horse-whim commenced work drawing water, and kept the Mine dry to the fifteen-fathom level for some time ; but as the works were extended, it was soon found that it would be indispensable to procure engine-power, and during 1847 a 30-inch cylinder, double action engine, with a supply of pumps, was obtained from England, and erected on the Mine, commencing work on 1st July, 1848. Shortly afterwards machinery was added for crushing ore, and for drawing or hauling ; and this engine, with a brief interruption, caused by the breaking of the main shaft in June, 1850, has been at work ever since.

" As the extent of working increased so did the water, and, in 1850, a larger engine was purchased and erected—commencing work in January, 1851. Both engines were employed in pumping for some years ; but, latterly, all the water has been brought to one shaft—now sunk a depth of sixty fathoms, to which level the Mine is kept in fork by the last-mentioned engine, which is of 36-inch cylinder, single direct action. The other engine is used in hauliing and crushing.

" In December, 1849, the first smelting furnace commenced work and was shortly followed by a second ; and, for some time, a large portion of the Ores were reduced to regulus before shipment.

" The great attractions presented by the gold-fields of Victoria during the year 1852, induced most of the men to leave. The smelting works ceased altogether on 17th March, and were not resumed till March, 1855.

"Nearly all the miners, also, left ; and it was with considerable difficulty the engine was kept going, and the Mine kept dry—at one time there were but four miners. During 1854, however, and especially in the early part of 1855, large numbers returned or came to work, and since then there has not been any material interruption.

"The Ores comprise almost every variety, as yellow ore, or pyrites, blue and green carbonates, muriates, grey and black sulphurets, oxides, bell-metal and peacock ores, and native copper, or malleable. The percentage also varies much, from 66 downwards.

"As to the present state of the Mine, the deepest level is sixty fathoms below the surface, at which depth it is kept drained. The deepest level in which tributers are working is fifty fathoms from surface.

"The underground workings are nearly all confined to the original section of eighty acres, No. 1271, extending nearly from North to South. Two other sections, Nos. 1284 and 1405, South of the original section, also belong to the Company, as well as a considerable portion of No. 1429, and some allotments northward—part of No. 1400.

"The engines on the Mine are as follows:—One 30-inch cylinder, 6-feet stroke, double action condensing, now used only for hauling and crushing Ores. One 36-inch cylinder, 8-feet stroke, single action, direct expansive and condensing, used only for pumping; those at present attached being a 12-inch plunger column, and drawing lift at the bottom ; between five and six strokes per minute keep the Mine in fork.

"Each of these engines has two large tubular boilers of about thirty feet by six feet, all of which were built on the Mine, as well as another spare boiler. One ten-horse power portable high pressure engine employed in turning, boring, chaff-cutting, &c., &c.

"There is also on the works, but not yet erected, one 50-inch cylinder condensing engine and a tubular boiler, in plates.

"One set of stamps and a plunger-jigging machine, for Ore dressing, to be erected immediately; one water wheel, and perpendicular and circular saws.

"The buildings now erected are—the two engine-houses and boiler-houses above named, with crusher and lathe-house attached, and draining case.

"A large and very substantial erection of stone, with slate roofing, just completed—and comprising engine-house, boiler-house, crusher, and mine stores.

"This is intended for the reception of the present drawing engine, as the ground around it is sinking. There is one metal foundry or cupola, one brass foundry, smith's shops, and iron store, carpenter's shop and timber yard, and saw pits, weighbridge and office, and a counting-house, with manager's residence attached, a commodious and handsome building. There are also residences for the accountant, clerk, agents, and engineer—and about thirty other cottages occupied by the workmen and miners; also houses for the pitman, timbermen, sumphmen, and a range of barracks, or changing rooms, for the miners; also a magazine for powder, store for candles, stores for Mine materials, stables, &c.

"At the smelting works there are five Ore-reducing furnaces, one Copper roaster, one refinery, Copper store, and Ore shed, all substantially roofed; also superintendent's residence and office, smith's forge; brick kiln, and brick shed for fire bricks which are made on the Mine, of very superior quality, from clay and sand obtained in the immediate neighborhood.

"Besides the drawing done by the engine, there are eight horse whims, two double whipseys, and several single ditto; and on the Ore floors are twelve jigging sieves, picking tables, &c., &c.

"The last return shows the number of hands employed, as follows :—

	Men.	Boys.
Officers, agents, clerks, overseers	8	—
Engineers, enginemen, stokers	10	—
Pitman, timbermen, tutworks, &c.	43	—
Tributers (raising ore)	106	23
Tradesmen, carters, laborers, kibble-fillers	82	13
Smelters and furnacemen	36	—
Masons (2), laborers, smiths, &c.	17	—
Total men	302	36

Besides a large number of woodcutters, carters, and others who are completely dependent upon the Mine for their means of subsistence.

"All the Ores raised are now reduced to fine copper before shipment; 595 tons were shipped in 1861. The expenditure during the year being £48,300; the greater portion of which is circulated on the spot for wages, fuel, &c. £8,713 was paid for fuel for the smelting works alone; timber being alone used."

The entire quantity of Ore raised from the commencment to the close of the year 1862, was 38,220 tons of 21 cwt., and of an average produce of nearly 20 per cent. The quantity raised during the past year was 2,940 tons, of an average of 16½ per cent. The quantity of fine Copper made during the year 1862, was 486 tons 12 cwt.

The total value of the Ore raised from this Mine has been above half a million sterling. The Kapunda Mine has been worked, on the whole, carefully and economically, and but little of the produce has been lost, which it would have been possible to save with the appliances at command. However, as the depth of the workings increases, and the average percentage of the Ore becomes less, it will be necessary to employ new and improved machinery for dressing the Ores of lower percentage than it has hitherto been thought worth while to deal with; and this course, I am informed, is about to be adopted, the Manager of the Mine having recently paid a visit to the Bremer Mine to inspect the machinery in use there, that mine being decidedly the most economically and thoroughly worked of any in the colony.

A large township (Kapunda) has sprung up near the Mine, and contains several substantial buildings, amongst others, four commodious places of worship, a Bank, a Mechanics' Institute, Post Office and Telegraph Station, Court House and Police Station; several Hotels, a fine Railway Station,—for Kapunda is now united with Adelaide by the iron road, trains running daily twice each way. There are a number of good shops and houses, and the population probably numbers altogether about 2,000.

Adjoining the Kapunda Mine, on the South, is another valuable mineral section, which was worked for a short time, but abandoned in consequence of the water coming in too strongly to be kept down by the appliances at the command of the South Kapunda Mining Company; the Mine, however, is believed to be quite equal to the Kapunda, and I understand it is intended to resume the workings.

There is said to be another valuable property to the North-East of Kapunda, and known as Stephens's Mine, but no amount of work has been done here.

The Karkulto Mine.

LEAVING Kapunda, we proceed in a northerly direction through undulating country, and amidst numerous farms, on our road towards the far-famed Burra Burra. After a ride of 10 miles we come to the small but prettily situated township of Hamilton, on the Light, and when we pass this the scenery becomes more monotonous. There is plenty of cultivation, but little timber, and the road lying between fences and presenting no remarkable or pleasing features to the eye, and being moreover nearly flat, travelling, especially with no other companion than a led horse, becomes tedious. Thirty miles from Kapunda we reach Apoinga, a *village* consisting of one public house, a Post Office, and two farm houses; the scenery here is an improvement upon what we have passed through, and is also superior to what lies before us. Four or five miles further we come to the Karkulto Mine in the midst of hilly ground of moderate elevation. This is a rather remarkable mineral property, for the indications of Copper were considered to be so good that the South Australian Mining Association (the Burra Company) and the Royal Mining Company, each purchased a large block of land here. Both parties went to work on their property; large and regular lodes were found; the walls were well defined, the underlay was satisfactory, and all the indications appeared favorable, but very little Copper was obtained. The ironstone and gossan did not, as was hoped, give place to Copper; still a little Copper Ore was occasionally met with, and the proprietors felt encouraged to proceed, especially as the iron ore could be sold as a flux to the smelting works, at a price which helped to pay the expense of raising. The Royal Mining Company, however, soon abandoned the workings, and eventually sold the property at a loss. The Burra Company are still continuing operations and a few tons of Copper Ore have been dressed up, to yield an average of from 16 to 20 per cent. of Copper. It is still the opinion of some practical men that the Karkulto Mine will ultimately prove rich in Copper, though as the depth at present reached is upwards of 40 fathoms, it will probably be necessary to sink considerably deeper before the desired result can be attained. The South Australian Mining Association, who cannot be accused of a wasteful expenditure in the development of their property seem to have had great confidence in the Karkulto, for they have laid out upwards of £30,000 in opening the Mine.

The Burra Burra Mine.

THE road from the Karkulto to the Burra exhibits no features worthy of notice. The "Monster Mine" is about 100 miles distant from Adelaide, a little to the east of north. It is situated on bald hills of the transition series, and about 150 feet in height from the surrounding country. The prevailing feature of the geological formation is limestone. The ground being soft and easily worked a tremendous amount of timbering has to be employed to secure the drives, and in going underground one walks through miles of these galleries, without seeing anything but timber, and in some places the passages have been so narrowed with these supports that a stout person would find some difficulty in squeezing himself through. There is less to interest the casual visitor underground at the Burra than there is in many other Mines far inferior in mineral wealth. A large quantity of the Ore consists of what is called "smalls" and this, as well as much of the other Ores, is so coated with the "country,"—or soil in which it is found,—that it would escape observation from the uninitiated. In proof of this I may mention that as I was going underground we came upon a pair of men, who had by them what appeared to be a large heap of rich loam, I remarked to my guide —"Capt. Dick that looks as if it would make good garden soil;" I thought at the same time there might be some Ore amongst it, but was surprised to learn that the pile had yielded, on assay, an average of 42½ per cent. of Copper. Here and there in the workings you may come upon a splendid bunch of red oxide and malachite, and the specimens of blue and green carbonates to be found in this Mine are extremely beautiful. It is a singular circumstance, but the miners agree in saying that there is not a regular *lode* in the Burra Mine, however, if there is no lode, there is plenty of Copper without it, the whole country being impregnated with it. The Burra appears to be one vast "pocket" full of Copper. Its original appearance in a huge boil on the surface was so remarkable that numbers of persons undertook the journey from Adelaide—quite an adventure to many in those days—for the mere purpose of seeing this wonderful deposit of Ore. A vast hollow is now shewn at one part of the Mine, about 100 yards in diameter and 30 or 40 feet deep, whence thousands of tons of the richest Ores were taken. This great hollow, however, is owing, perhaps, as much to the sinking of the ground because of the large amount of excavation which has been performed in following the Copper below. The Ores obtained from this Mine have been chiefly red oxides, very rich blue and green carbonates, and malachite. Native Copper has also been found. Many very beautiful specimens of all the varieties named have been procurable from the Burra Burra, and are to be seen ornamenting the mantlepieces or cabinets of an immense number of houses in the colony.

To proceed with a brief history of the Mine; it was discovered by a shepherd named Pickitt in 1845, and in order to secure the fee simple of mineral land it became necessary to purchase a special survey of 20,000 acres ; paying the Government for the same in specie. The survey was taken on August 16th, by Messrs. C. H. Bagot and G. F. Aston on behalf of themselves and others, afterwards called the Princess Royal Mining Company, and by Messrs. William Allen and Samuel Stocks, Jun., for themselves and others, who afterwards became incorporated with the South Australian Minning Association, which name is still borne by the Burra Company. These two parties were called respectively the "nobs" and the "snobs," the former representing the "aristocracy" of the colony, and the latter the merchants and tradespeople. The nobs were unwilling to combine with the snobs in a joint stock company for carrying on the Mine, and therefore although they united to purchase the ground,—as neither party could, unaided, raise the hard cash—as soon as the survey was completed, the land was divided by drawing a line through the centre from east to west. Lots were then drawn for the land, and the "snobs" became the fortunate proprietors of the northern portion of the survey, and on which the Burra Mine existed. The Princess Royal property was ultimately sold for pastoral purposes at 18s. an acre.

The first Directors of the S. A. Mining Association, and who were appointed to manage the affairs of the Burra Mine, were Messrs. Charles Beck, James Bunce, John Benjamin Graham, John Bentham Neales, William Paxton, William Peacock, Christopher Septimus Penny, Emanuel Solomon, and Samuel

Stocks, Jun. Mr. Henry Ayers was appointed Secretary. Operations were commenced immediately, the number of miners employed being ten, under the superintendence of a Captain, and with a smith to sharpen and repair the tools. The first shot was fired on the 29th September, 1845, blasting a large mass of rich Ore, and in a short time several drays were loaded for the Port. The workings were carried on with vigor, and the produce of the Mine surpassed the most sanguine expectations entertained on its discovery. The original working capital of the Company was only £1,500; but with a Mine so rich and so easily worked that amount proved sufficient, until the sale of Ore increased the funds available for working expenses. During the first six years of the history of the Burra, nearly 80,000 tons of exceedingly rich Ore were raised and shipped to England, yielding a profit to the Company of £438,552; a pretty good result from an original outlay of £10,000 for the land. At the close of the first six years since the opening of the Mine, the number of hands employed was upwards of 1,000; but at this time the newly discovered gold-fields in Victoria attracted a large proportion of our population, and especially the miners, who left in such numbers that only 100 were left at the Burra—the Kapunda Mine suffering in like manner; indeed, I believe at one time only five or six men remained at Kapunda, including the Captain and Purser. This state of things produced a serious check on the working of the Mines; at the Burra, where pumping engines had been erected, the machinery was of necessity stopped, and the water let in; the comparatively few men who remained being employed in working above the water level. For the greater part of three years the Mine continued thus, the Government then took the matter into their serious consideration, and rightly deeming the prosperity of the colony to be dependent, to a great extent, on that of its Mining interest, they adopted measures for the introduction of a number of Cornish miners. When these immigrants arrived, the water was pumped from the Mine, and full operations were resumed, and have been carried on with comparatively trifling interruptions, until the present time. The greatest number of hands employed, was in 1859, when it amounted to 1,170 persons. The discoveries at Wallaroo, two years ago, caused some of the miners to remove to that locality, and several were attracted by the reports of the great richness of some of the Mines in the far North. In November, last year, also, a still larger departure of miners took place, in consequence of inducements held out to them by a certain Coal Mining Company in New South Wales. Prior to this time, however, the working of the Mines at Wallaroo and in the far North had tended to raise the rate of wages, and it was deemed advisable by the Directors of the Burra to confine their operations to those workings above the 55-fathom level; the water was therefore let into the lower part of the Mine—from the 70-fathom level to the 55—and it is found that at the present rate of wages, larger proportionate profits can be realized, without incurring the expense of pumping and working the lower levels. I may here allude to a rumor which is frequently circulated, and occasionally with increased vigor, that "the Burra is nearly worked out." I have heard this rumor repeated almost annually, for the past fourteen or fifteen years, and I think the best answer to it, is a reference to the continued prosperity of the Mine. With a disposition on the part of some to spread or to countenance such a report, it will readily be believed that the occasion of letting the water into the lower workings gave a fresh opportunity to the croakers; but, after careful enquiry, I see no reason to doubt that the Burra will continue to yield large quantities of rich Ore, and consequently to pay good dividends for many years to come. The yield of Ore has ranged, for many years, from 10,000 to 13,000 tons a year, the produce of the Ore giving an average of from 22 to 23 per cent. of Copper; or about 2,500 tons of pure Copper, when smelted, and yielding to the colony an average annual amount of at least £225,000. The total amount expended in the colony by the Burra Company, up to the present time, is about £1,700,000, of which upwards of £1,000,000 has been paid in wages. The gross profits amount to £850,080, of which £714,560 have been divided among the shareholders, and £135,520 added to the capital stock, while £10,560 remained undivided.

It may not be altogether out of place to mention the rate of wages paid at the Mine. It is subject to fluctuation according to the state of the labor market, and the Burra Mine perhaps pays a trifle below the average paid at some other Mines, as it is reasonable to suppose a concern so well established and so substantial might do, because the men can reckon with certainty on permanent and regular employment. It is true they can now do so at several other Mines, but I merely throw this out as a suggestion explanatory of the alleged fact. Laborers' wages have varied from £1 5s. to £2 per week. Miners' from £1 15s. to £3. Mechanics from £2 2s. to £5 12s. per week. Boys from 9s. to 15s. per week.

The surface workings present a very animated appearance. The great engine for pumping the Mine is of 80-inch cylinder; the water raised is made available for working other machinery, turning large water wheels, or being conveyed over the mine by means of landers. The jigging shed is a long erection and contains a large number of jiggers for washing the Ore. Cornish stampers are worked near at hand by means of a waterwheel, and reduce the Ore preparatory to its being washed. Until a comparatively recent date a large quantity of Ore in fine particles ran to waste, being washed into the creek; it is now found worth while to wash this refuse, and a number of men are employed at it,—I believe on a kind of tribute wages, i. e. being paid so much in the pound for the value of the Ore they clean; and I am informed they do very well at this work. It is calculated that the quantity of refuse, the accumulation of many years, in the Burra Creek is worth many thousands of pounds sterling.

The Mine is under the able superintendence of Capt. Henry Roach, who has managed it very much to the satisfaction of his employers for about 15 years. He has under him a whole staff of grass captains and underground captains, and other officers.

There are several townships in the neighbourhood of the Mine, the two principal being Kooringa and Redruth; next in importance is Aberdeen, but this is connected with the adjoining (Bon Accord) Mine. There are also the suburban townships of Hampton, Little Hampton, and Copperhouse. Kooringa and Redruth contain six places of worship, belonging to the Wesleyans, Independents', Church of England, Bible Christians, and Primitive Methodists. There are also two Banks, several public houses, one first-class hotel, and many shops and other buildings, but altogether the townships present a miserable and dirty appearance. I must not omit, however, to mention an Hospital connected with the Mine, and a Telegraph Station and Post Office united, the latter being one of the best buildings in the place.

In concluding my notice of the Burra Mine I may, perhaps, be allowed to introduce some clever lines, written soon after its discovery by J. W. MacDonald Esq., then Acting Colonial Treasurer.

These lines describe pretty accurately what actually occurred on the discovery of the Burra Mine, and with little or nothing of a "poet's licence":—

> Have you not heard of the Monster Mine?
> There's never a man to be got to dine,
> There's never a clerk who will pen a line,
> At my behest or thine.
> They are all gone forth to the houseless North
> To gaze on the Monster Mine.

> Have you not seen the solemn Nobs?
> Have you not marked the eager Snobs?
> Have you not heard of the wiles and jobs,
> Of the men who can't *combine*?
> With a snobbery, nobbery, jobbery, bobbery,
> All for the Monster Mine.

> See how hurriedly they come and go,
> Backwards and forwards—to and fro—
> Making a sad and solemn show
> Of the human face divine;
> They wear not a shirt but has lain in the dirt
> Three nights at the Monster Mine.

> E'en "Teddy,"* who is the *grinding* man,
> Has mustered his *paper* all he can,
> He's mustered his baggage—pot and pan.
> Ah! where shall the great man dine?
> He's cut his stick in a coach and six,
> To tread on the Monster Mine.

> He's closed his desk, he's locked his till,
> He's taken his great fat brother "Bill,"†
> And a member of Council greater still.‡

---

* Edward Stephens, Esq., then Manager of the Bank of South Australia.
† W. Giles, Esq., then Manager of the S. A. Company.
‡ Captain Bagot.

Ah! where shall the great men sleep?
They shall shiver all night in waistcoats white,
And long for the morning's peep.

They shake they shiver, they shiver they shake,
They have no Dolly their beds to make;
It behoves the great men to be wide awake,
When the Snobs and fleas *combine*.
Ah! Snobs and fleas would ye dare to teaze
The King* of the Monster Mine?

Up spake the King with solemn frown,
"The very best *strata* are beds of down,
'Tis meet a King should wear a crown,
'Tis meet a King should dine;
Then, 'Billy,' poor fellow, may bluster and bellow,
But where is the Monster Mine?"

The Snobs they are hurrying up and down,
Some lend them a sovereign, some a crown,†
They leave not a shilling in all the town
To pay for a pint of wine;
Then steady, boys, steady, the Company's ready,
Hurrah! for the Monster Mine.

Quoth Nob, "Are you ready?" quoth Snob, "I am;"
But the Company shut to the door with a slam;‡
Yet the Company's paper was nothing but sham,
When the moon began to shine,
For it shone through the paper like a shadowy vapor,
But not on the Monster Mine.

Then away with all rancour, and jabber, and jobs,
The Snobs and the Nobs, the Nobs and the Snobs,
The "lords of the soil," with *Dicks* and *Bobs*,
Their brotherly arms entwine;
And long may the Snob and his brother Nob
Grow fat on the Monster Mine.

The Princess Royal Mine.

THIS Mine strange to say was in reality discovered before the
Burra, and it was owing to its discovery that the Burra was found
shortly afterwards. It is also a singular fact that the Princess
Royal Mine is situated near the South-eastern corner of the
special survey, and the Burra just within the North-western boundary. Four hundred shares were issued by the Princess Royal

* A title bestowed upon Edward Stephens, Esq., because from his position as
Manager of the Bank he ruled the movements of the other parties.

† It is an actual fact, that in order to raise the required amount (£20,000) in hard
cash, for the purchase of the special survey, money was scraped together in every
possible way, and so small a sum as one sovereign was borrowed to help to
make up the amount.

‡ The Manager of the S. A. Company, endeavored to secure for the Company a
share in the Mine; but he could not provide *hard cash*, and the Bank Manager refused
to discount his drafts on the Company in London, hence the Manager was reported to
have left in a huff.

Company, and the amount paid up on each share was £34. The working of this Mine was commenced nearly at the same time as that of the Burra, and with considerable success. A great quantity of rich Ore was raised and shipped to England, the average percentage of Copper being above 27. A large parcel made over 29 per cent. The workings were carried on until the year 1851, when the water was cut at about the 30-fathom level, and the capital of the company being all expended, as well as the proceeds of the Ore,—in machinery, buildings, wages, &c., &c., the shareholders lost heart and determined on abandoning the Mine. The land was subsequently sold, and enclosed for a sheep run, the price paid being £9,000 for 10,000 acres. The total proceeds of the Ore raised were above £7,000, and the Mine ultimately paid a dividend of about 13s. in the pound on the original cost and outlay. The shares, however, at one time rose to above £200 each. It is not at all unlikely that if a company were to recommence working this Mine in a legitimate way, and with the determination to sink £20,000 or £30,000 at the outset and look for no return beyond what would pay for the labor employed for twelve months, the Mine might yet prove to be one of great value. Its comparative proximity to a shipping port is greatly in its favor, for cartage can be had for about £2 10s. per ton.

The Bon Accord Mine

Is situated so close to the Burra, that from a short distance the buildings and workings of the two mines appear to belong to one establishment. The land on which the Bon Accord Mine is found was purchased by a Scottish Company, now known as the Scottish Investment Company. Its close proximity to the Burra first led to the ground being taken up; and I believe there were some slight indications of the existence of Copper. A considerable amount of work has been done and a large sum expended on the Mine. Favorable indications have appeared to warrant the outlay, and some of the piles of stuff which have been raised look as if they would almost pay for dressing, they are so impregnated with particles of Ore, amongst which may be detected red oxide and black Ore. The engine-shaft is sunk to a depth of 50 fathoms and there is a large cross course which, it is thought, will probably intersect a lode of Ore. Other shafts have also been sunk on the property, and a considerable length of drives has been opened underground, but without any very satisfactory result. This company really deserve to be more fortunate, for the steady perseverance with which they have worked on in spite of discouragement.

Some mineral sections have been taken out about 20 miles North of the Burra, but I am not aware of any Mine that has been worked to any extent in that direction.

However, a little to the West of North, and from 22 to 28 miles from the Burra, we come upon a batch of Mines on the Broughton River, and hence called

The Broughton Mines.

THE indications here were very promising, and some fine rich Ore was obtained, but the country was so hard that it was found it would not pay for working, and after a few months the Mines were abandoned. An attempt has been made lately, on the representations of one of the miners, who is willing to embark his all in the enterprise, to recommence working one of these Mines ; this man declares that the country, in the particular Mine which he wishes to work, is not too hard to be worked with profit, considering the rich lode of Ore which exists in the Mine ; and it is not unlikely that another trial may be made here. These Mines are situated on a very fine sheep run belonging to the Messrs. Fisher.

There is but little timber in this neighbourhood, and the country presents no features of special interest either to the geologist or to the artist; the ground is for the most part undulating. Some of the hills are rather rugged and rise to a height of 200 or 300 feet, and are occasionally covered with the abominable spinifex, or porcupine grass, a vegetable production which no animal will eat, and which is considered utterly useless. It does not, however, grow here in such rank luxuriance as it attains in the far North, where, in some places, it is quite an impediment in the way of horses travelling, the plants growing to a large size, and the spines being both sharp and strong. However, on these fine runs this porcupine grass is the exception and not the rule, and we travelled over many miles of splendid sheep country, until we came to Boowooley (pronounced Bowley), one of Mr. H. B. Hughes' stations, also in the midst of beautiful pastoral land. From Boowooley to Charlton the appearance of the country improves, and some parts are very beautiful. I should suppose no finer sheep runs are to be found in the colony than those I have named, though there may be others equal in value. As we approach the Rocky River we see belts of finely timbered land, gums, pines, and other trees growing luxuriantly. Here we observed that singular variety of the wild duck called the wood-duck, which possesses the power of perching on the boughs of trees like birds of flight ; the feet of these wood-ducks are only half-webbed ; they are elegantly shaped birds (for ducks) and their plumage is beautiful.

In the neighbourhood of the Rocky River the country is very fine, and many large and handsome gum trees add to the beauty of the scene. After a ride of above forty miles we reached White Park, a station belonging to the Hon. George Tinline and William Fisher, Esq., and where I was most hospitably entertained. This station deserves to be called a park from the beauty of its scenery, and the fine clumps of noble gum trees studded over the gracefully sloping hills. A creek of excellent water runs through the property, and its course is marked as is usually the case, by a continuous line of gum trees.

The road from Charlton to Mount Remarkable is, in many parts, exceedingly pretty. Now you ride along the banks of the creek, commanding an extensive view over fine undulating country, and presently a turn in the road leads you up a narrow gully where you can see nothing but the steep hills on either side. Within a few miles of Mount Remarkable, the trees for some distance present almost the appearance of an avenue, but nearer the Mount the land becomes more thickly timbered, and scarcely so interesting to the eye. Here and there an agreeable variety appears, as for instance at the residence of G. B. Smith, Esq., S.M., where the land becomes more open, and the presence of a fine creek of water has its effect upon the size and appearance of the trees. After a most agreeable ride of about 15 miles, I arrived at Mr. Smith's, who received me very kindly, and at whose house I remained for a couple of days.

Mount Remarkable presents a fine appearance from this place, being distant about two miles. It rises boldly to the height of 1,857 feet above the surrounding land, and is rather more than 3,000 feet above the level of the sea.

The Mount Remarkable Mine.

ABOUT the year 1846-7 Copper Ore was discovered in the neighbourhood of the Mount, and a special survey of 20,000 acres was taken out by a few adventurers, money having become more plentiful than when the Burra was purchased. Prospecting parties were employed, and £3,000 was spent in preliminary operations; some tolerable Ore was found and a small quantity sent home as a sample, together with a mineral supposed to be Emery, but the Copper lode was small and "pinched," and the ground very hard, so that the workings were abandoned nothing worth the name of mining having been done. When the discovery was first made, like many others, it was very much puffed, and Mount Remarkable was spoken of in Adelaide as a "Mountain of Copper," just as some hills farther North are now represented to be. Strange to say, however, the survey did not include the hill, but stopped at its southern base. The company was ultimately wound up and the land sold at a low figure, it being in those days thought a remote settlement, 175 miles from Adelaide. The survey is now probably worth over all more than double its original cost, £1 per acre.

The Spring Creek Mine.

THIS Mine is situated on the Northern end of Mount Remarkable, one of the high peaks of the Flinders Range, and is about 11 miles from the township of Melrose, which is at the South side of the range. The Mine is about 35 miles from Port Augusta, and is, as its name imports, on the banks of a fine perennial creek of excellent water. The hills on either side are from 300 to 400 feet in height, and very steep, so much so, that in an ordinary dray—which, by the bye, is a heavy vehicle—eight bullocks can only draw 15 cwt. of Ore to the top. Notwithstanding this difficulty at the outset, parties offered to contract to cart all the Ore from the Mine to Port Augusta, at thirty shillings per ton; but with a trifling outlay a better road could easily be cut. The Mine itself is on the East side of the creek. A bold reef of rocks running up the face of the hill contains numerous stains of Copper, and on breaking off portions of the rock where these stains occur, Ore is almost invariably found; in some cases blue and green carbonates, but more frequently the richest red oxide and ruby ore, and sometimes a little native Copper. A small drive of about 2 fathoms has been made about 120 feet above the level of the creek into the hill, and shews several veins of red oxide from one to six inches in thickness and running down, as if to a main lode. I was informed that from this place five tons of Ore were sent to England as a sample. The appearance of the "country," where the ground has been opened, is favorable for Copper; there is a good deal of ironstone on the back of the reef of rocks, and also fine gossan, and several tons of rich Ore might be quarried from the face of the hill. Opinions differ as to the probable permanence of this Mine, some asserting very positively, that no continuous lode will be found, and that when what is now visible on the surface is removed, there will be an end to the Mine. Others, on the contrary, are as confident in their belief that the Mine will prove both rich and lasting. Without venturing to give too positive an opinion myself, I may state one or two circumstances which, I think, favor the probability of a good Mine being developed here. It is situated in a decidedly mineral country; the other end of the range, or Mount Remarkable proper, containing deposits of Copper Ore, at a direct distance, it is true, of eight or nine miles from the Spring Creek Mine; but beyond Spring Creek, about three quarters of a mile to the West, and over the next range, another discovery has been made, and a claim taken out by Messrs. Nott and others. This claim consists chiefly of grey oxide in thin veins, but little has been done as yet to prove the ground. The reef of rocks, in which the Ore at the Spring Creek Mine is found, runs, as I have before said, down the face of a steep hill, and points North and South, Messrs. Nott & Co.'s claim being nearly due West of it. This would indicate the continuance of a course of Ore in that direction, though I cannot go so far as to say that at present the lode has been distinctly traced between the outcroppings of Ore. The proprietors, however, believe that it does exist. Some parties who speak depreciatingly of the Spring Creek Mine, do so, I believe, because of the extreme richness of the surface Ores and for no other reason, but this is not, in my opinion, a sufficient reason. The geological features of this colony present occasional anomalies, and many of the ordinarily received rules are found sometimes to be disregarded by Dame Nature. It does not always follow that where there is a rich surface deposit there is nothing beneath. I confess I incline to the opinion of a very intelligent gentleman, who has had considerable experience in mining in this colony, and who remarked to me respecting another Mine—" These surface deposits must have boiled up as it were from below, and even if we cannot find a *continuous* course of Ore as we go down, we shall no doubt find it again in depth, but people here either have not capital, or have not patience to go deep enough." The deepest Mine in the colony the Burra Burra, is only about one-fifth of the depth of some of the Copper Mines of Cornwall, and there are only about two dozen other Mines where anything more has been done than what would be called "surfacing" in Cornwall. Persons of experience in English mining will therefore at once see that the development of the mineral wealth of this colony is but in its infancy.

To conclude my notice of the Spring Creek Mine, I think it highly probable that if an adit were driven South into the hill, it would lead to a discovery of importance. I shall look forward with great interest to the development of this Mine, as likely to set at rest some disputed questions in relation to Mines and mining in the North.

Great Gladstone Mine.

PROCEEDING northwards from the Spring Creek Mine through about 20 miles of fine country, well grassed and lightly timbered, we come to the Great Gladstone Mine—named after the Chancellor of the Exchequer. This Mine is situated on a bank rising to the westwards towards Mount Brown—another high peak of the Flinders Range—the country to the East being flat. The distance from Port Augusta is 32 miles. The surface indications of the existence of Copper here are favorable. The country consists of clay slate, and quartz, and several outcroppings of Ore and Copper stains are found in many places. The back of the lodes consists chiefly of ironstone, and a considerable proportion of iron is found in most of the Ore raised. There are, however, some fine specimens of rich Copper ore, grey oxide, and brown ore, besides green carbonates and a little malachite. Other metals also exist in this Mine, small particles of Galena being met with, and another metal which I believe to be Silver. Probably careful research might lead to other discoveries. Three shafts have been sunk, from 8 to nearly 17 fathoms, and a considerable extent of ground driven, from which a large quantity of mineral has been raised. I say mineral, as it would not be strictly correct to call it Ore, though there is a good deal of metal amongst it; but without machinery much of it would not pay for dressing. However, as producing mere curiosities for the cabinet this Mine is one of the richest in pretty specimens ; the crystals of quartz stained with Copper and other metals being very beautiful. The ground is soft, scarcely any necessity existing for the use of powder, and a large amount of work has been done at a very moderate outlay. There is a considerable extent of ground on the Great Gladstone Company's property yet untried, and where the surface indications are encouraging; it is, therefore, not improbable that future researches may result more successfully than those hitherto made. Should a payable Mine be found here, its situation will give it many advantages; its nearness to a shipping port, and also to Melrose, the inland township of Mount Remarkable, and its immediate proximity to sheep and cattle runs.

After leaving the Great Gladstone Mine we had the assistance of a guide, who undertook to take us a short cut to Kanyaka, and by which, he said, we should save a distance of 20 miles. We accordingly started, our guide shewing the most utter contempt for roads ; but I often wished, despite the supposed saving in distance, that we were on the beaten track, for we crossed the Willochra Plains, which consist of loose sandy soil covered with stones as if road metal had been sown there broadcast ; moreover the ground is full of holes made by little animals, which abound here, and the holes being about four inches in diameter, and perhaps a foot in perpendicular depth, the travelling was very unpleasant for the horses as well as for the riders. Here we " camped" in the middle of the day, to refresh man and beast, at the junction of the Willochra and Pitchiritchie Creeks, amongst beautiful native flowers, including sweet peas. There was good water and feed for the horses. We saw a number of native fowl which, at a short distance, appeared very like domestic poultry, and were supposed by the " new chums" of the party to be so. After discussing some bread and meat which we brought with us, and resting our horses for an hour, we again proceeded on our journey, remarking how very much such an exhibition as we then made would " take" in London—five men, rigged out in bush costume, and with pannicans, hobbles, saddle-bags, &c., three of us leading pack horses,—but, *mirabile dictu*, not one smoker in the party! Really it would not be a bad idea for some Albert Smith to give an exhibition, by means of *tableaux vivants*, of life in the bush of Australia. The ground by no means improved as we proceeded, and as we had lunched, or camped rather early, the afternoon was long and tedious. During the journey we saw innumerable kangaroo rats, " wideawakes," (a variety of the wallaby), a few kangaroo, and some fine turkeys. Towards evening we approached Kanyaka, and saw a very remarkable rock, which, at a little distance, appears to rise abruptly from the plain. This rock, which is on the bank of a creek, measures about 22 feet in height from the plain, but where the earth has been washed away on the creek side, it is fully ten feet higher, and is about 30 feet long and 18 or 20 feet through. There is a waterhole in the creek so nearly corresponding in dimensions to this rock that many persons fancy it was by some extraordinary convulsion thrown out of the bed of the creek. It is a hard kind of granitic rock. The natives in the neighbourhood appear to attach some superstitious notion to the rock, for they manifest an anxiety, when at the point of death, to be brought and laid down to die under its shadow. I was informed that their wishes in this respect are not merely attended to by their companions, but that the course pursued by them is by no means unlikely to hasten the desired end. The unfortunate native is laid down under the big rock, with his blanket or opossum rug, and a very small supply of provisions, his comrades then retire to the distance of a mile or more, where they encamp, and come to the rock about once every twenty-four hours to ascertain if the sick man is still living; if he is, a little water and food is given him, but scarcely sufficient to support existence, so that before many days he attains his wish, his death no doubt having been expedited by exposure and insufficient food.

Kanyaka, the station of J. B. Phillips, Esq., is rather prettily situated ; a gum creek runs past the station, and contains good and permanent water in pools. After a thunder storm I have seen it present the appearance of a small river. The hills, especially on the east side of the gully, are bold and lofty, and there is sufficient timber to relieve the country from the appearance of barrenness. The grass also, at the time of my visit, was very luxuriant and looked inviting to the scythe. The station comprises several substantial stone buildings, and a fine stone woolshed is built about 300 yards from the houses. One of the offices is used as a Post Office, and the number of letters and newspapers passing through it is surprising, considering the scattered population of the North, and the nature of their occupations. About a mile from the station, rather to the south of west, a Mine has been discovered amongst low hills, and is called

The Kanyaka Mine.

THE country consists chiefly of pipeclay, decomposed slate, and soft sandstone, and is very easily worked, from 25s. to 35s. per fathom being the price paid for sinking or driving. The softness of the country, however, will necessitate the employment of a quantity of timber for the purpose of securing the shafts and drives. There is a very well defined lode, having near the surface the appearance of indurated clay, strongly stained with Copper, and containing occasional stones of ore of from 20 to 30 per cent. I should judge that for some distance the whole produce of the lode as raised would be worth from 7 to 10 per cent., but of course it can be dressed to a higher yield. As the lode goes down there is an improvement in the quality of the Ore, and I saw two piles containing seven or eight tons, which had been dressed to an average percentage of 30. Several stones of the ore (grey oxide) would probably yield 50 per cent. of Copper. Since my visit, and up to the present time (January 28), the quantity at grass is about 20 tons of 30 per cent. Ore. The lode is from two feet to thirty inches in width, but is rather too flat, dipping from the horizon only about two feet in the fathom. A great deal of gypsum is found at the sides of the lode. A very fair amount of work has been done here, several shafts having been sunk, the deepest of which is 15 fathoms, and these are connected by drives extending for about 40 fathoms, and proving the lode to be of the character I have described over a large extent of ground; it has been traced altogether for 11 chains in length on the surface. I have no doubt this Mine will prove a paying concern, from the small expense at which it can be worked, and the moderate cost of cartage—which can be obtained to Port Augusta (distant 57 miles) at 35s. per ton—and there is a good quantity of Ore in sight, the lode continuing very regular. The lode in this Mine is most easily distinguishable even by the untutored eye, the country being nearly white and the Ore of a dark blue and grey color. A company is engaged in working the Mine (on Section 1533), the superintendence being given to Captain Tonkin. The shares are at a premium.

The Mount Craig Mine.

FROM Kanyaka and the neighbouring Mine we proceeded to the Mount Craig Mine, a property that promised very well, and from which some very fine Ore was raised; but, owing, probably, to mismanagement somewhere, the Mine was abandoned, and the Company wound up. The Mine is situated favorably enough, and in mineral country. There is a creek with precipitous banks running through the section, and from these banks drives have been made with the view of cutting the lode; but they appear to have been made parallel with the lode, instead of at an angle with it, and as two parallel lines can never meet, it is no wonder the lode was not cut. One of the best educated and experienced mining captains we have has given me his opinion that there is still a good Mine on the property if it were properly worked, and I have no doubt the same remark would apply to many abandoned claims. A great deal of work was done here, but no results of importance were realized, and for want of capital to carry on further operations the Mine was abandoned.

The Wirrawilka Mine

Is embedded amongst hills, about two miles North of Mount Craig, and where the Company have seven sections. The indications of Copper are plentiful and extensive; but the ground is hard in some places. Eleven shafts have been sunk, the deepest being nearly 30 fathoms, and a number of drives have been made, of which the longest is 50 fathoms; but no result has yet been attained to compensate for the outlay. The hills on the property are very steep, and shafts have been sunk, in some cases, close to the sides, and from a considerable elevation. Ore has, in many cases, been found all the way down. The quantity raised, in proportion to the amount of work done, is small, and past results are not very encouraging for further operations. Nevertheless, some pretty samples of Ore have been raised, and some specimens of red oxide were obtained from the lowest level. In some parts of the property regular lodes have been met with and followed to some depth, consisting of quartz, gossan, and felspar, and containing some good stones of Ore. The country, for several fathoms, consists of a porphyritic rocky stratum, and beneath this clay slate is met with. This is a favorable indication, and it is possible that at a greater depth the country may become more settled, and better results be obtained. At the time of my visit, about 30 men were employed on the Mine, but since then the number has been considerably reduced.

I examined some claims in the neighborhood of the Wirra-wilka, and which were represented to me as very rich; but my sight cannot have been so good as that of the person who took out the claims, for I could see nothing to warrant even the expense of the first application for the land. There were some stones dug out from near the top of a high hill, and which were stained green, but I could not call them Copper Ore. There was no lode, nor anything favorable in the way of indications, *except* the green-stained stones. I do not wish to identify these claims by any more minute description, but I allude to them to show how sanguine some persons are if they find anything the color of Copper Ore.

I heard of two men (shepherds I think) in the North, who rather unaccountably gave up their situations, and were missed for some time; about a month afterwards, a person who knew them discovered them in a secluded spot, working most industriously, digging up ironstone. They had saved money enough to purchase a stock of tools and provisions, and thought by working quietly and alone to raise Ore enough from their Mine to enable them to retain their supposed wealth to themselves. The person asked them what they had got there? They replied, " a Copper Mine, and a rich one too, see it is just the color of penny pieces;" but they looked rather crest-fallen when they were told that their Mine was worthless, and their Ore would not make penny pieces at all. It appeared they had never seen Copper Ore, but having heard of its existence, they took out a claim of ironstone, in mistake, and worked it for a month!

The Kirwan Mine

Is situated about four miles South of Mount Craig and 72 North-east of Port Augusta, at the foot of a range of hills of moderate elevation sloping towards a plain to the westward. The country consists of a soft light killas and a kind of pipeclay. There are several lodes and branches of Ore on the property, running generally to the East of North, and underlying from 18 inches to two feet in the fathom. Three shafts have been sunk, the deepest of which is 21 fathoms, and at the bottom of this shaft there is a lode between three and four feet wide and composed of quartz and copper pyrites. A level has been driven on the course of one of the lodes about ten fathoms into the hill, and a cross-cut about five fathoms, cutting several branches of Ore running into the lode. Another cross-cut has been driven to the South-east, cutting a lode of fine blue and green carbonates about a foot wide; several tons of good Ore have been raised here. A short distance to the West two shafts were sunk on the course of the lode, which is composed of carbonates of Copper, intermixed with ironstone, and is traceable for 300 yards. A quantity of

D

Ore was also raised at this part of the workings. On another section, about a mile and a-half South-east of the first-named place, a small shaft has been sunk on an east and west lode which produced some fine grey and red oxide.

The country on the Kirwan Mine differs somewhat from that on either side, and would seem to be a band of more favorable strata for copper. It is a very promising looking Mine.

The same proprietary have another Mine in the neighbourhood of Arkaba, which, as it belongs to the same company, and is known by the same name—the Kirwan Mine—may be described here. It is on the Messrs. Marchant's Arkaba run, and about 80 miles north of Port Augusta. The country consists of killas. There is a good East and West lode of fine black and yellow Ore, about two feet wide, and underlying about 15 inches in the fathom. A shaft has been sunk six fathoms, and a level driven about five fathoms from the surface on the course of the lode. This level is driven eastwards about ten fathoms. Another lode, or propably a branch of the same, lies about ten feet to the North, and contains good stones of Ore on the surface. Some tons of Ore, averaging about 40 per cent., have been raised here, although comparatively little work has been done. Water and timber are plentiful on the section and in the neighbourhood.

The Napoleon Mine.

From the Kirwan, we rode along the foot of the hills for about seven miles further, through mallee scrub and loose sandy soil, until we came to the claims of the Napoleon Mining Company, and here, I regret to say, I was disappointed; I had heard so much of the richness of these claims that I was surprised to find nothing but the poorest indications. A hole had been sunk about 10 or 12 feet, through country consisting of carbonate of lime and felspar, and containing a few specks of Ore, but the appearances were most unpromising. I enquired of the person in charge where the fifteen tons of Ore were to be seen which I was informed had been raised, and was told that there never was so much, and all that had been obtained had been carried away as specimens! I was further told, that that was the best of the Napoleon Mining Company's claims, but that there was another seven miles off, to which my informant offered to accompany me if I wished to go; but as he assured me there was not a particle of Ore to be seen, I declined to ride 14 miles for nothing, on a hot day, through a miserable country. On my return to Adelaide, I was annoyed to find that this person having had a quarrel with his employers, purposely misled me; and I ascertained from them that the section seven miles further was that from which the Ore had been raised, and that which I saw was one which they thought of abandoning. I can, therefore, give no account of the Napoleon Mine. I may, perhaps, be allowed to say that the reports of the Mine written by the person alluded to are strangely at variance with his statements to me, and in them he speaks of lodes of rich Ore, and expresses the highest opinion of the property.

———

From the Napoleon Mine we proceeded to Warcowie, a station of P. Butler's, Esq., and rather prettily situated. There appeared to be some very good country on this run, although, as we rode over a large portion of it by moonlight, it was not easy to form a judgment; still we could, in many places, distinguish a fine crop of grass growing. After partaking of the customary hospitality of the station, we laid in a stock of flour, meat, tea and sugar, for the next three days, and started to visit a mineral claim (No. 1665) S.W. of Rawnsley's Bluff. We rode about nine miles through undulating and nearly flat country, with occasional patches of light scrubby timber, but for the most part monotonous and uninteresting. The claim is situated on low, undulating, settled ground; a strong reef of ironstone shows on the surface for 250 or 300 yards, and contains some good stones of green carbonate of Copper. I consider the indications favorable, but as the discovery was quite recent, no ground had been opened. From the appearance of the surface and nature of the country I should not be surprised to hear of the development of a good Mine in this place.

Being directed where to find water for ourselves and horses, we proceeded about three miles in an easterly direction, and came to a fine spring, where a well had been dug in the bank of a creek, and about six or eight feet from its bed, the water overflowing into the creek. Here we camped for an hour and a half, kindled a fire, boiled our quart pots, and having made tea, "did ample justice" to the provisions we carried with us. There was a little good feed for the horses, but they appeared rather dainty and did not make the most of it, as no doubt they would have done could they have foreseen what was before them, for they were without food for the next 33 hours, and then got but a scanty supply. Our guide now designed to take us another of his "short cuts," which he accomplished pretty much in the same way as if he had travelled along three sides of a square instead of one; starting nearly at right angles to the direction which we had to go. We soon came on to rough, desolate-looking, country, dry and parched, as if—as is possibly the case—no rain had fallen there for years. The land was stony, and as dusty as a road over which heavy traffic passed; not a blade of grass was to be seen, yet there was some kind of vegetation, miserable stunted scrub, which only rendered the appearance of desolation more complete;

even this scrub, though retaining the semblance of vitality, seemed dried up and sapless, and the branches broke almost like rotten wood. A double portion of the curse seemed to rest on this miserable place, and as we came to an opening, revealing miles of similar country to our gaze, we could not help thinking of the "blasted heath" in Macbeth; and it would have required the art of a witch to have found water there to boil, or sticks fit to make a fire. The country I have thus feebly attempted to describe is on the edge of the Eastern Plain, and on the boundary of a run, at the other side of which is one of the finest portions of country in the North. Still we travelled on, for there was no use in stopping, and our guide seemed to entertain a vague and uncertain notion that there was the bare possibility of our finding a suitable camping place before night, and feed for the horses. About half-past 6, we reached Yudnapunda Springs, where there was a good supply of excellent water, but not a bite of any kind for the horses, we therefore tied up the poor brutes to let them rest, after giving them drink ; we then lit our evening fire, made "johnny cakes" of flour and water, which we baked in the ashes, where also we grilled some chops, and having made tea we endeavored to enjoy the sumptuous repast. For my part, and I believe others shared my feelings, I felt distressed on account of the poor horses, and could enjoy nothing. The ground about the Yudnapunda Springs was quite a "Golgotha," covered with numerous skeletons of unfortunate cattle starved to death, and which had come to the water to drink and die. Many other springs in the North are surrounded by similar relics; for some three or four years ago there was a very dry season, and sheep and cattle perished by thousands in this part of the country. After resting two hours, we rode on through similar dry, dusty, barren country, for two hours more, when, as there seemed no prospect of improvement, we came to a halt for the night in some horrible mallee scrub ; hobbled the horses, to give them a chance if there should happen to be any feed near, but they were tired, and immediately lay down, and we soon followed their example. I selected a soft place in the sand, and spreading my wallaby rug on the ground, rolled myself up, and was quickly asleep. We rose early the next morning, and made a cup of tea, with water carried in canteens ; and having breakfasted off johnny cakes, started at about half-past 6. The horses had wandered about a mile in search of feed, but found none, and they looked very miserable. After riding some miles along the edge of the plain, through similar country, we began to turn a little in towards the hills, in order to reach a "gap," the only spot our guide was acquainted with, where we could get through the tremendous range that frowned down upon us. However, since he last travelled in the North—some two years previously— another gap had been discovered, and if we had known of that we should have had a better road and 20 miles shorter. I don't know then that our guide would have preferred it, for he seemed to delight in great circle sailing, and also in selecting the roughest route for travelling. This cannot have resulted from anything of the poetic in his composition, or from any love of the sublime and beautiful, for he appeared to revel in the rugged and the desolate. Poor fellow! I could not help feeling sorry for him; for the uncertain seasons, and vicissitudes of sheep-farming, in the North, had helped to ruin him, and perhaps he brooded over his misfortunes, and a morbid feeling took possession of his mind, making him like to wander over barren and desert country.

I have dwelt rather long over this part of our journey, in order to give some idea to those who "sit at home at ease," of what bush life often is. The reader may imagine, to some extent, from what I have described, what our brave explorers have to encounter, when for weeks together they have, day after day, a repetition nearly as bad as what we endured, and without the saving clause of plenty of food and water for themselves. Our horses alone suffered, and that for only two days.

But to finish this part of the narrative: my horse was taken ill and knocked up, and for some four miles I had to drive him before me. Towards noon we reached a creek containing good water, where the horses drank and rested for about twenty minutes. 1 managed to get my horse along for three miles further, when we camped for two hours, and the poor animal seemed in a dying state. However, we drove him on four or five miles, after he had rested, and then were obliged to leave him. After a tedious ride of three hours more, we reached Angorigena, the station of H. C. Swan, Esq., where I was very kindly received, and my companions proceeded about four miles further, to the Blinman Mine.

The next day I went to look for my horse but could not find him. Our guide, who was an experienced bushman, then kindly undertook the search, and tracked him for six or eight miles, through some of the wildest country imaginable—over rocks, and along the sides of almost precipitous hills, where no one would suspect any but wild animals of venturing. However, the horse could not be brought back, and was left at Wirryalpa, on the Eastern Plain.

Proceeding from Angorigena through moderately hilly country, lightly timbered at intervals with pine, I came to the

Wheal Blinman,

A MINE belonging to the Yudanamutana Mining Company. There is a large reef of indurated clay slate, intermixed with iron-stone and gossan, and forming the back of a lode running nearly North and South, and distinctly traceable for about 200 yards on the surface. In the clay slate small pieces of green carbonate and grey ore are found. The lode runs to the top of a hill, about 90 feet in height from the creek, and here it forms a large "boil," in which the ore was discovered. On the rocks being broken away a fine lode of exceedingly rich Ore was seen, 8 feet wide, and underlying westwards into the hill about 18 inches in the fathom. When I visited the Mine the top of the hill was being stoped away, and a splendid course of Ore was exposed to view. It was nearly solid metal for a width of 8 feet, and had a peculiarly brilliant appearance, like a mixture of grey and red oxides. Some rich green and blue carbonates were occasionally met with, and specks of the finest yellow ore, known as " semi-metal." At the time of my visit No. 1 Shaft was sunk nine fathoms on the course of the lode from the top of the hill, and carried ore the whole way down. No. 2 Shaft is about 8 fathoms south of No. 1, being further into the range, the first shaft commencing very near the face of the hill; the same lode has been cut in this shaft, where it is from 8 to 10 feet wide, and the shaft sunk about 5 fathoms on the lode; the ore raised is of similar quality to that in the other shaft, and the quantity raised is about 100 tons of first and second quality, and 150 tons to be smelted. About 18 fathoms farther south No. 3 workings are going on, and which, at about two fathoms below the surface, have produced five tons of the finest Ore, and about 10 tons for smelting. About 10 fathoms still farther south, on the same lode, a shaft has been sunk four fathoms, from which about five tons of second quality Ore have been raised, and a few tons have also to be reduced to regulus. About 20 fathoms north of No. 1 shaft another shaft (No. 5) has been sunk four fathoms through a good gossan lode containing Ore of first and second quality. Fifty tons of Ore of all qualities have been raised from this shaft, and 20 fathoms farther north No. 4 shaft is sunk to a depth of 10 fathoms through a good ore-bearing lode from three to four feet wide. At the depth of eight fathoms the lode inclines farther west, and a drive is being carried to intersect it, and when it is cut again drives will be carried both North and South, on the course of the lode, under the various workings above-mentioned.

Up to the close of 1862 above 600 tons of Ore of all qualities were raised here, 400 of which were estimated to yield an average produce of 40 per cent. A fine block of this value, and weighing about 2½ tons had been sent to Port Augusta for shipment. The country was very dry, a well having been sunk 20 fathoms in the bed of the creek without cutting water. There are, nevertheless, some fine springs in the immediate neighbourhood. A number of substantial pine huts for the miners have been erected on the Mine, besides a good store of galvanized iron with a cellar beneath, also offices and Captains' apartments. The distance of this Mine from Port Augusta, by the present road, is about 140 miles, but a new road has been cut through the Brachina Creek, and by which a saving of about 20 miles would be effected, and a better road secured for feed and water for cattle. The rate of cartage paid has been from £4 10s. to £5 per ton, but should the season continue favorable, and feed be plentiful, it will probably be much lower shortly.

Mr. Davison's Claims.

FROM the Blinman we went to look at some neighbouring claims, the first was No. 1683, taken out by Robt. H. Davison, about 2 or 2½ miles from the Mine. This contained good indications, reaching from the gully for some distance up a steep hill, and a small pit had been sunk near the foot, disclosing a lode of Ore of fair quality. Ore was also found in two or three other places which were opened, and the section was altogether a promising one. At the next claim we visited, a small shaft was sunk 15 fathoms through whitish clay slate, following stains of Copper down from the surface. This work was performed with commendable diligence, by only two men, in a very short space of time, but my own impression of the indications was that they were not sufficiently encouraging to warrant the expenditure of labor bestowed on the work. However, it was singular to find continuous stains for so great a depth, and some persons of experience in mining recommended the industrious workmen to persevere. I have been since informed that they found some small pieces of grey ore in the bottom. The ground was certainly such as " Copper would live in," as the miners say, and it is not impossible that a course of Ore might be met with at a greater depth.

We next proceeded to Messrs. Chambers & Finke's Station of Moolooloo, where we passed the night. There was in the hut an armchair of peculiar construction, quite unique in fact, being cut and hollowed out of the solid trunk of a gum tree, even the seat of the chair having been left in its original position as part of the solid tree, and showing the perfect round of the trunk. The wood was cut away underneath to reduce the weight, but it was nevertheless rather heavy. The design was ingenious, though the workmanship was not quite such as a cabinetmaker would turn out, and the chair did not exactly come under the denomination "easy."

The next morning we rode to Patawarta, formerly called Mount Rugged, to see a mineral claim. The country we rode over was the most beautiful I had seen since leaving Mount Remarkable, indeed I think it surpassed anything I saw in that neighbourhood. The land was at that time well grassed, and our road lay sometimes over undulating ground and sometimes through wild and rocky gorges, the hills rising like high walls on either side. At last, passing through a fence in a narrow gap between two such hills, we entered a kind of "pound"—that is a tract of land so surrounded by high and rugged or precipitous hills that a few yards of fencing across the gap sufficed to confine the cattle in an area of several square miles. There are many such "pounds" in the North, but the grandest of all is the Wilpena Pound, and this will be described in its proper place.

Having entered this pound a beautiful view presented itself; on the right was a fine bold range rising to a height of about 500 feet, and so steep that though not impracticable, few cattle would ever attempt to cross it. There was a little vegetation on it, just sufficient to relieve the prevailing reddish-yellow of the rocks and soil covering its side, while a creek containing many fine gum trees skirted its base. On the left, and rising gently from the bank of the creek, were fine grassy slopes studded with clumps of elegant pines, giving the place the appearance of an English park; while to complete the picture, in the background the bold dark rocky summit of Patawarta (distant about two miles), towered majestically above the surrounding hills. Proceeding in the direction of Patawarta we gradually ascended until we came amongst high hills, and rather "disturbed" looking country, scantily covered with scrub. On two of these hills we found claim No. 1654.

This claim contains several lodes, having backs of ironstone protruding above the surface, and showing a good deal of grey carbonate of Copper and yellow Ore. Copper is found scattered in many places over the section, and the lodes are traceable over two hills and a gully, for a distance of nearly a mile. Some very good specimens of Ore have been found here, and Bismuth of a high percentage has also been discovered; it is, therefore, very probable that the claim may prove to be a valuable one. Adjoining sections have been claimed by Mr. R. Williams, Mr. W. Rose, and others; and the indications afforded are such as to warrant, at least, the expenditure of some labor in testing the place.

I afterwards visited several claims in the neighbourhood of Wheal Blinman; but, as I said in the introductory chapter, I do not intend to describe every separate claim which I saw, and I shall, therefore, pass them over with a brief notice. Some of these sections exhibit very promising indications, and I may mention, especially, two taken out by Mr. Swan, and others by Mr. Martin and Mr. Gaedechens. Mr. Campbell, also, has two claims about four miles from the Blinman, and which contain Copper Ore. Another claim about two miles North-East of the Blinman, and called

The Wheal Butler,

DEMANDS a rather more particular notice, from the peculiarity of the Ore which it yields: a reddish brown or liver-colored Ore, which, on assay, produced 37 per cent of Copper, although most persons supposed it to be merely a variety of ironstone, which, indeed, I believe it is; but so largely impregnated with Copper as to make it worth working. Two sections have been taken out here (Nos. 1391 and 1392); they are on low undulating ground, and in settled country. A good lode passes through both sections, and has been opened, at intervals, for nearly a quarter of a mile. The back of the lode consists of ironstone, micaceous iron, gossan, and quartz; and, below these, stones of green and blue carbonate, and a quantity of liver-colored Copper Ore are found. The underlay is about 2½ to 3 feet in the fathom, and pits have been sunk to various depths—4, 8, and 12 feet—proving the regularity of the lode, which varies from 18 inches to 3 feet in width.

Leaving the Blinman in the afternoon we made a short stage and camped at Owanegan, formerly the head station of McKinlay, the explorer, and at that time (1850) the most distant station from Adelaide—about 300 miles in a direct line. At Owanegan there is another pound similar to that which I described near Patawarta; the approach to it is very fine. The traveller proceeds up a gully between bold rock-capped hills, the space gradually narrowing, and the hills becoming more precipitous, until he enters a gorge or gap only a few rods across, and here, as usual, there is a fence with a sliprail. Shortly after passing the fence, there is a mass of rocks on the left hand, which, viewed from the other side, bears a striking resemblance to an old man's face, and it has been named accordingly. Some stunted gums and pines appear "in the place where the wool ought to grow," and pines and scrub adorn the shoulders and bust of this natural sphinx. I should have said that pines and occasional gum trees grow in great abundance at the entrance to and also within the pound. We made this station in the full expectation of finding abundant feed and water for the horses, and in the former we were not disappointed, but there was no water, and every sign of the old well was obliterated, floods having come down the creek had evidently filled it up. A trough was there, washed down from its original position, but it was not until some time had elapsed that a well was discovered in another place, about 15 feet deep and with a puddle of water in the bottom. There were, however, no means of drawing the water; at last a pine pole was put down, and our indefatigable guide, who, to do him justice, was equal to any emergency of this kind, descended the pole with a canteen and pannican slung round his neck. It was now nearly dark, and as the water was only two or three inches deep it was difficult to scoop it up, those on the top therefore threw down lighted bits of paper to illuminate the well, and at last the canteen was filled and brought safely up. Meanwhile two of the party, not knowing where the others were, had kindled a fire in the hut, so that the quart pots were soon boiling. When I took mine off I observed a peculiar frothy scum on the top, and on examination found it to be the larvæ of the mosquito, with which the water was quite thick; fortunately most of them had floated, but the tea retained rather a *soupy* flavor—it may have been more nourishing, but it was certainly not more agreeable for this addition. However, hunger and thirst demolish fastidiousness of palate, and we made a good meal and turned in, watching the

E

stars through the gaps in the roof. During the night a thunder storm came on, accompanied by tremendous wind, which threatened to blow the remains of the roof off, and rain which gave us the benefit of a shower bath. The next morning we were astir early, and made a start in order to reach water where we might breakfast. At a short distance from the hut we came upon a "bushman's grave," that of Mr. Walter Gill, a gentleman with whom, some years before, I had the pleasure of a slight acquaintance. The sight of a grave is calculated, under any circumstances, to call forth serious reflections, but in the solitude of the bush it awakens those feelings with tenfold force, and there is something peculiarly affecting to stand over a lonely sepulchre in the wilderness, far removed from the haunts of men. I saw a few others during my travels, but none so neatly enclosed, or with such pretty surrounding scenery as this. I made a sketch of the place, and proceeded on my way after the rest of the party. The scenery for some distance was equal to any I had met with in the North, the land being well timbered and with a greater variety of trees than usual. Passing under Patawarta, the view was such as would have delighted an artist, the grand old mountain, with its summit of overhanging rocks, rose high on our right, while ranges of hills stretched away in the distance. There were what appeared to be one or two small caves in the face of the hill, which was covered with rocks and scrub. On our left the hills were of less elevation and more gentle slope, and covered with pines, sheaok (casuarina), and gums. A belt of pines also grew at the foot, and partly up the slope of the mount, while the foreground appeared like a wide smooth and well gravelled carriage drive. Between the mount and the hills, on our left, was a "gap" leading away into the distance, and through which we saw other hills beyond, forming a pleasing background to this beautiful picture. Patawarta is visible from Mount Remarkable, a distance of about 170 miles.

After a ride of above three hours, we came, at 9 o'clock, to a good spring of water in a creek, where we gave the horses drink, and filling our canteens proceeded further, before breakfasting, in order to find better feed for the animals ; the land, in immediate proximity to water, in the North, being generally bare of grass. As we rode on we came to some rather open country with rocks—a kind of ferruginous clay slate—here and there on the surface, and amongst some of these we found a curious fissure about 20 feet in perpendicular depth, at which point it took a slight turn and went still deeper. Some hills at a little distance presented a peculiar red appearance, and were composed of stratified rocks, probably, stained with iron. We saw Mount Tilley to the left, in a heavy black looking range, Mount MacFarlane on the right, Mount Hack, straight before us, and Mount MacKinlay and Mount Uro (or Huro), a little to the right, in the distance. We were now passing through Mr. Field's run. Presently we came to Mr. John Baker's run (Pernunna), and passed through a gap in the range ; on our right there was a mass of rocks full of small caves of peculiar appearance, and one of which had a regular porch, with one pillar at the outside corner—two sides of the porch being open, besides the entrance to the cave. On our left, were the Cock's-comb and the Mount Hack ranges, enclosing a "pound" about half a mile wide by ten miles in length, extending in a westerly direction to Sliding Rock Creek.

I must not omit to mention the remarkable form assumed by many of the hills in the North, and hence called "reap-hook ranges;" one side rises abruptly, and culminates, generally, in a knob of rocks, while the other side slopes away gradually in a graceful concave form, very much the shape of a sickle.

We were delayed three days at Mr. Baker's station, by the rain—a most unusual circumstance in the North, where it rains seldom, and when it does, a thunder shower, lasting for half an hour, often floods the country for miles. So uncertain and limited is the quantity of rain in this part of the country that it has been facetiously remarked, the northern squatter's rain guages are constructed so as to indicate a fall of *fifteen drops to the square mile*. The effects of brief and sudden thunder storms soon pass away, so that a steady rain of several days was hailed with delight; and at this time the effects proved most beneficial and lasting, for the rain continued, with occasional intermission, for eight consecutive days, and extended over a tract of country comprising, probably, 30,000 square miles. The creeks were set running, and large waterholes were filled with a supply, which, without further replenishing, would last for years. In any future remarks that I may make about the luxuriance of the herbage, it must, therefore, be borne in mind that the season, when I was privileged to travel in the North, was an exceptional one. The grass sprang up rapidly after the rain, and in less than three weeks country which before had presented the most barren and desolate appearance was covered with a rich carpet of emerald green.

The Mount Huro Mine.

DURING our stay at Pernunna we paid a visit to the Mount Huro Mine, distant about two and a half miles. This Mine is situated in rather disturbed country, and amidst high and rugged hills. A heavy reef of quartz and ironstone, on low hills gradually rising from a creek, is found on examination to contain strong stains (green and blue) of Copper, with occasional small pieces of Ore, and in one place we found some good specimens of grey oxide. Nothing has been done to develop this Mine, and it is just one of those places about which it is difficult to express an opinion; it may prove a valuable property, if the surface indications lead to a good Copper-bearing lode, but this has yet to be proved. From its position and distance from a shipping port it would require to be very productive to be a paying concern. The same remark will apply to many other Mines in the North.

When we left Pernunna we found that the rain had made a great alteration in the ground over which we had to travel. We had frequently to dismount and lead our horses, to enable them to get the more easily through the loose boggy soil. Our road through the Malkio Gap was very rough. We were obliged to ride for some distance along the bed of the creek, which was now running strongly, in some places nearly up to the saddle girths, and was very rocky, so that the horses had difficulty in keeping their footing. We came presently on to more open country, surrounded by hills in the distance; here we saw some red kangaroo—as red as a fox. I noticed that the prevailing color of these animals, in the North, was a reddish fawn of various shades, whereas that of the kangaroo in the Southern and Eastern districts of the colony is generally a mouse color. The uro, or huro, is a variety of the kangaroo distinguished chiefly, for its skin being covered with hair, while the common kangaroo has a wooly kind of fur; I fancy it is also more graceful in form, and it attains a larger size than the kangaroo, uro being frequently seen six feet high, and sometimes taller. Another peculiarity is that it lacks the strong claw on the middle of the hind feet; probably to adapt it better for the rocky country in which it lives, and where the long claw might get broken. Hence a uro does not rip open the dogs like a kangaroo, though he often hugs them severely. I have heard of a uro carrying off a kangaroo dog in his arms, while two others were hanging on to his flanks with their teeth; I was also told of a gentleman being seized and carried for a short distance by one of these powerful animals.

As we rode across the open country I observed, several miles distant, in an easterly direction, something which presented very much the appearance of a large factory chimney. On looking at it through the glass it proved to be an immense mass of flat-faced rock in a range of hills, and just the shape of a tall chimney stack. This morning we saw some remarkable deposits of ironstone—containing, probably, above 80 per cent. of metal—in immense masses, outcropping on the surface to a greater extent even than any of the Copper Mines I have seen. There was one hill which had a huge iron cap overhanging its brows like one of the new-fashioned "helmet hats." Of course these vast deposits of iron, 200 miles from a shipping port, must remain unavailable until the discovery of coal enables the metal to be smelted on the spot; and even then greater facilities for cartage must be provided before any profit could arise; but I shall have more to say on both these subjects bye and by.

As we proceeded we passed Constitution Hill, and saw the Mine (?) named after it. The section is on gently rising ground at the foot of the range, and a reef of limestone runs through it containing some slight stains of Copper and a few small particles of grey oxide.

A short distance further brought us to Mount Serle, a fine massive mountain between 3,000 and 4,000 feet above the sea level, and rising almost abruptly from the surrounding country. This part of our journey was through better land than a great deal that we had seen, and the scenery was very passable, though not remarkably interesting. There was a fair sprinkling of light timber and scrub, and a short distance from thr mount we observed, nailed to a tree, a board containing the following important announcement—"Water up the creek, to the left, both salt and fresh." Some benevolent individual had taken the trouble to cut out the letters so that they should not he easily obliterated. Obeying the directions, we found plenty of good fresh water where we camped, and not standing in need of salt we made no further search. A few miles more and we arrived at Messrs. Scott & Kingsmill's station of Owieandana, where we stopped the night, as the weather was threatening and we could make no other station on our road for a distance of 30 miles. In the early morning some heavy rain fell, but the day was pleasant for our journey.

About five or six miles from the station, we came to

The Mount Rose Mine.

THE working of this Mine having been temporarily stopped, I had no means of descending the shafts. Before I left Adelaide I was given to understand that there was a person in charge ; otherwise I might have made arrangements for going underground ; but no one was there, and all the ropes, &c., were removed. I also ascertained that the water was in the lower part of the Mine. However, I did the best I could, and examined the ground and the piles of Ore at grass, and looked down the shafts, in which the lodes were plainly to be seen. Judging from the Ore and the nature of the country, as well as from the appearance of the lodes, so far as they were visible, I formed a very favorable opinion of this Mine. The killas and gossan were of the right kind, and the country appeared to be easy to work. Although the best of the Ore raised had been carted away to the amount of nearly 100 tons, several tons remaining at grass would quite pay for dressing.

As I consider this Mine as likely to become one of considerable importance, when the working of it shall be resumed, I have procured the following brief particulars relating to it from a gentleman who visited the place shortly before the cessation of operations. I may first state that the Mine is 215 or 220 miles from Port Augusta, and a good road exists between the two places :—

No 2 shaft is above 13 fathoms in depth. The lode has been stoped away North from this shaft for two fathoms and a half, and is more than three feet wide, of solid black and grey Ore of high percentage, and which is standing seven feet high in the North end of the stopes. No. 3 shaft is sunk 10 fathoms, on the underlay of a large counter lode, five feet of which have been cut through, and only one wall found at present. A few feet were driven on the course of the lode, and a branch or leader of fine Ore, 18 inches wide, was cut in the bottom of the level. No. 4 shaft is sunk to the depth of 10 fathoms, and contains a quantity of Mundic, also a lode two feet wide and composed of green carbonate of Copper, mixed with ironstone and gossan. This lode is parallel with that in No. 2 shaft. The Ore shipped to Swansea was assayed by Messrs. Bath & Co., there, and yielded a produce of 28¾ per cent.

About three miles further we came to the

Apex Hill Mine,

SITUATED in rather rough country and amongst steep hills. There is a lode traceable for about 150 yards on the surface, and running about North-east and South-west. The back of the lode consists of ironstone with quartz and copper ore. The country is quartz and killas, or clayslate. Several stains of copper are found in other places away from the lode; there are very strong green stains on the face of a precipitous rocky hill at one side of the creek, while the hill on the opposite side is covered with blue stains. The Ore in the lode is not very rich, but looks promising, consisting of green and blue carbonate with a little grey Ore. It is impossible to say what it may prove in depth, the ground not having been opened at all.

————

At the time of my visit a beautiful creek of excellent water, and shaded by fine gum trees, ran purling amongst the hills, and on my return, three weeks afterwards, the water was still abundant. We found plenty of native peaches here, but they are so soon attacked by a kind of caterpillar, or maggot, that it is difficult to meet with a ripe specimen that has not been commenced on by one of these tiresome insects. The peach is about as good a fruit as any of the wild fruits of the colony, and makes a very nice preserve, though it is rather insipid in its natural state; nevertheless it is very refreshing to the traveller in the bush, and has been made the means, occasionally, of sustaining life for days together when no other fruit was to be found. The stones are hard, round, and full of small holes, and when cleaned are of a yellow color; they are extensively used for making bracelets and breast pins, mounted either with silver or gold.

Having gathered a quantity of these peaches we made some jam in one of our quart pots, and ate it with Johnny cakes at our midday meal. On this occasion our horses fared as well as ourselves, for they had an hour and a-half's rest on as good feed as they could wish for, and they needed it, for they had 50 miles to travel to day. However, the road was good and water plentiful, and we kept the beaten track after leaving Apex Hill, and this enabled the horses to travel better, for they seem always to prefer the road to the bush. We met 250 or 300 fat cattle, looking very clean and sleek, and presently afterwards saw a snake 5 feet in length, the first that we had met with. The country through which our road lay was more interesting than the average of what we had passed through, and as we felt we were on the last day of our upward journey, we were in good spirits, and rattled over the last 30 miles between half-past two and half-past seven, at which time we reached

The Yudanamutana Mines.

WE met, during the afternoon, about 20 drays loaded with Ore from these Mines, and carrying, altogether, about 50 tons. This sight tended very much to enliven the road, and the magnificent quality of the Ore showed us that we were approaching a Mine of no ordinary character. On one dray we saw a splendid block of Ore estimated to weigh at least four tons, and containing, throughout, about 40 per cent. of Copper. The prevailing Ore was grey oxide, accompanied by some green carbonate, and a few beautiful crystals of arseniate of Copper. Another dray, in company with the former, contained two large blocks, which, together, must have weighed above three tons. These, we were informed, were originally part of the same block as the first mentioned.

The last 40 miles of the road was, with a trifling exception, excellent, and it would be no difficult matter to drive tandem at a good pace nearly all the way. The exceptional part of the road (Compass Pass), however, can be avoided by taking a new cut leading more to the eastward, near Illinawurtina, Mr. John Scott's station, and this track is considerably shorter. I was amused, when riding alone past Oomberatina, a station of Mr. Elder's, 15 miles from Yudanamutana, by some natives who called out to know if I was "going to look for Copper?" The blacks now quite understand the object of many of the whites who visit the North, and several of them have pointed out Copper Ore. A blackfellow was the first to discover the Yudanamutana Mine, which he called "Big one old man Copper"— "old man" being an expression in use among the blacks to denote anything of full size, or maturity, and when "big one" is prefixed the superlative degree of comparison is understood.

When nearing the Yudanamuntana Mine we came to a fine gum creek, the windings of which we followed for some little distance until, passing through a gorge, we entered a romantic looking spot surrounded by high peaked hills, for the most part crowned with rocks, in some of which the stains of Copper were visible from a considerable distance. The situation of the Mine reminds the traveller of Swiss or Welsh mountain scenery, and several fine sketches might be taken of the neighboring hills; indeed, a panoramic view of the locality would be very pretty. The creek is shaded by gum trees and shrubs, the latter being seven or eight feet in height; and the hill sides are covered with low scrub and small flowering shrubs, with here and there a clump of pines. The first grand discovery which was made here consisted of a large boil of Ore in ironstone and gossan, on the top of a low hill in the midst of the surrounding amphitheatre of mountains, and I have frequently observed a similar formation in connection with Mines in the North. The hill referred to in the present case is on section "135A," and is about 80 or 90 feet above the creek, which flows on two sides of its base.

The boil of Ore at the top contained altogether about 70 tons above the surface, a portion of it, on one side, is still left standing as a sample or memento of its original appearance. When an inspection of the Mines of the colony was made by order of the Government, although no report was published, it was generally understood that such report would be rather damaging to most of the Northern Mines, and it was stated that the Yudanamutana Mine, especially, was condemned, the boil or bunch of Ore on the surface being said to be all that ever would be found there, as it went down suddenly in the shape of a wedge, and ran out, and that no more than 60 tons could be raised from the hill. This assertion—which, whether it formed a part of the report handed in to the Government or not, was much talked of out of doors—has been most triumphantly refuted by the subsequent development of the Mine. It was to a certain extent true that the great mass of Ore, which was 10 or 12 feet wide, did go down in the shape of a wedge for a few feet, but the *end* of the wedge has not yet been reached, though shafts have been sunk on the lode to a total depth, from the top, of 28 fathoms. The aptness of the comparison ceased after the first two fathoms, for a finer and more regular lode below I never saw. The Ore in the lode varies from two to four feet in width, the walls are of killas, and the lode of fine gossan and steatite, with splendid grey Ore, accompanied by green carbonate and liver-colored Ore. The lode underlies about one foot in the fathom, and has been traced altogether for above two miles in length, occasionally cropping out on the surface. On the property of the Yudanamutana Mining Company the lode runs for a mile, and has been proved at intervals for a length of above 1,300 yards. The principal workings are in the neighborhood of the boil of Ore on the hill, where a shaft (No. 2) was sunk at the side of the lode for 11 fathoms, proving the lode to that depth, the country as well as the lode in the bottom looking very favorable. Several fathoms to the north of this shaft were stoped away from the surface, so that the nature of the lode could be plainly seen. Some stoping had also been done on the south side of the hill with a similar result; and a very promising counter lode to the east of the main load was opened for a length of between 20 or 30 feet, and a few feet in depth. At the bottom of the hill on the South, an adit level (No. 1.) was being driven on the course of the lode; from the mouth of this level the large blocks of Ore, before referred to, were taken; a winze was sunk three fathoms at the entrance to the level, and the appearances presented in it were highly satisfactory, the finest possible country with beautiful Ore in the bottom. A little further south, and across a small flat, 70 fathoms from No. 2 shaft, we find No. 1 shaft sunk 12 fathoms on the same lode, and in every respect looking as well as the other, several fine stones of grey Ore of about half a ton weight, and from 40 to 50 per cent. produce, were raised from the bottom in my presence. On section "135B," to the South of that which I have described, workings were commenced about 600 yards from No. 2 shaft, and several tons of red oxide and steel grey Ores raised. At this spot there is a curious volcanic looking boil of ironstone, and what appears very much like lava and scoriæ. This boil was hollow internally, so that while one of the miners was working here with his pick, a mass suddenly fell inwards into the cavity, nearly causing him him to fall with it. A short distance to the eastwards a branch lode has been cut, apparently converging with the other at an acute angle towards a point in the gully to the north, and about this point a cross course, from the west, seems to be intersecting the main lode. If this should prove to be the case, a large deposit of Ore may be looked for at the point of junction. I have now described the extent of the workings at the time of my visit, but I also inspected the adjoining mineral sections belonging to the Company, and on all of which Copper is found. Two of these (Nos. 285 and 1398) appear to be better than the others, and I am glad to learn that operations have been commenced on 285, called the Martichudina, and very encouraging results met with. On one part of this section there are large masses of rock containing Copper Ore in abundance, and in another place, stones of the size of road metal are scattered thickly up the slope of the hill for a width of 18 or 20 feet, and nearly half of them contain Copper Ore, many of them to the value of 40 per cent. A similar surface deposit occurs on section 1398, though perhaps not quite so rich as on 285.

I have been favored with the following additional particulars respecting these Mines by Henry Martin, Esq., the indefatigable Superintendent of the Company in Adelaide, and who has just returned from his third visit to Yudanamutana, he having visited both the working Mines of the Company three times in seven months. The total quantity of Ore raised at the Blinman and Yudanamutana togther, is estimated at 2,400 tons, and this has been accomplished by less than 80 men and boys in little more than seven months, in addition to a great deal of preliminary work, such as building huts, sinking wells, &c. Six hundred and thirty-eight tons of Ore, averaging at least 40 per cent. produce, had been carted from both Mines up to 22nd January, and 514 tons shipped at Port Augusta. Nine hundred tons are at grass at the Yudanamutana Mine, of which 300 tons are estimated to produce 50 per cent. of Copper, and the remainder above 25 per cent. Nearly the same quantity is at the Wheal Blinman, and is thus classed :—above 60 tons about 50 per cent.; 500 tons. 25 per cent., and 300 tons 15 per cent.

Several sections adjoining those of the Yudanamutana Company, and containing Copper Ore, have been taken out by other parties ; some of these claims are supposed to contain a continuation of the Yudanamutana lodes, and others may prove well worth working, but at present little or nothing hss been done to develop them, and therefore a detailed account of them is not strictly within the scope of the present work. However, I may state generally, that this part of the country is, for miles in extent, the richest in mineral of any I have yet seen, and when greater facilities are enjoyed for working the Mines and carting away the Ore, there will no doubt be many good claims opened in this neighbourhood. As the natives express it—" Big one Copper sit down all about."

On one of these sections (1685) taken out by Mr. Robert H. Davison, there is a rather singular waterfall—a very rare thing in the North. This fall—Petalinkina (" moonshine water") as it is called by the natives—comes over the side of a range about 200 feet in height from the gully, and, for 150 feet, quite precipitous ; indeed, half way up, a mass of rock overhangs a few feet, causing the water which trickles down from above to dash over in spray. A nice pool, about 35 feet in diameter and 4 feet deep, receives the water, which falls about 150 feet from the top of the hill, and then trickles down, amongst large rocks, into a second pool, 12 or 15 feet below. In another section (No. 1410), South of the Yudanamutana workings, and belonging to Messrs. Neales, Whitington, and James, there is another waterfall, very inferior in height, being not more than 20 feet, but far superior as to the surrounding scenery. The water flows along a narrow gully, between steep rocky hills, from 250 to 300 feet in height, and having their sides covered with porcupine grass, and pine and gum trees. There are several large and deep waterholes in this gully, and of considerable depth, so that the supply of water (of excellent quality) is unfailing, or, to quote our friends the natives, "never tumblef down"—this expression signifying death or dissolution. They also apply their favorite phrase to this place, "big one old man water—never tumble down." Near the end of the aforesaid gully there is a peculiar formation ; masses of rock rising, perpendicularly, to a height of 60 or 70 feet, and with a face almost as smooth as the sides of an immense jar, encircle nearly two-thirds of an eliptical basin, whose longest diameter is 100 feet, and its shortest 60 ; but in the upper side a huge cleft exists in this mass of rock, nearly corresponding in slope with the sidess of the hill behind. Through this cleft, and under a rude kind of natural bridge, composed of large blocks of stone, and having a little tree growing at one end, the water rushes, and dashing against a jutting piece of rock rebounds a few feet, when again meeting with a (slighter) resistance, it falls into the pool. When I saw this romantic little cascade, the rate of the fall was, I should think, about 100 gallons per minute, and the greatest depth of water in the pool was said to be 14 feet. The water continued to run from it, down a rocky gully, until it reached the main creek flowing past the Yudanamutana Mine. Before leaving this neighborhood, I may perhaps be allowed to describe a claim belonging to the "Welcome Copper Lodes Company," No. 1632, and which the proprietors, in commemoration of my visit, did me the honor to name

The Wheal Austin.

THIS section is half a mile South-South-West of the Yudanamutana Mine, and the country presents similar features, both geologically and physically. An immense reef of ironstone rocks runs up a rise from the gully in a North and South direction, and is evidently a continuation of the great Yudanamutana lode. This reef of ironstone and gossan contains strong stains of Copper, and numerous stones of green carbonate and grey oxide ; it is from 18 to 20 feet in width, and its course very regular ; it is without doubt a champion lode. At the South corner of the same section a good course of Ore exists, and the country contains a large quantity of Copper.

The Yelda Mine

The Northern Mineral Association have a very good section to the South-West of the above, and on the opposite side of the creek ; this they call, after the native name, "Yelda."

It is on a rather steep hill, nearly 300 feet in height ; a fine regular lode is visible on the surface for above 300 yards, running

S.E. by E. down the face of the hill, which is covered with scrub and porcupine grass. There are also two other secondary lodes running parallel with the main lode.

I also examined several other claims belonging to the same proprietary as the Wheal Austin, and all of which exhibited something more than mere good indications; there were regular well defined lodes on all the undermentioned sections, and it is highly probable that the whole would prove payable when worked, but unless some special features in the different localities demand notice, I shall pass over with a few brief remarks those on which no work has been done. Sections 1619, 1635, and 1674, are about a mile and a quarter E.N.E. from the Yudanamutana Mine, and show good lodes, and stones of Ore of a high produce, scattered over the surface. From these claims I proceeded, in company with Mr. Alfred Frost, to some others, distant less than 12 miles in a direct line, but to reach which, we had to perform an extremely rough journey of more than double that distance. I may mention by the way that Mr. Frost claims, and I believe justly, to have discovered more mines than any other individual in the colony. He is an excellent bushman, is capable of enduring great fatigue and considerable physical exertion, and is, moreover, a perfect enthusiast in mining matters; lest, however, this expression should be misunderstood, I must do Mr. Frost the justice to say that during several days which I spent in examining mineral sections, in many of which he was personally interested, I did not find that he had exaggerated in any statements which he had previously made to me respecting them. While speaking of Mr. Frost, I may also mention Mr. Burtt, who has for some time been associated with him in mineral discoveries, and who has also been so fortunate as to find several valuable mines; all that I have said respecting Mr. Frost will apply equally to Mr. Burtt, and having travelled for some days with this gentleman, I may say that I found him a most agreeable and intelligent companion. *Revenon à nos moutons*, as the French say. Accompanied by Mr. Frost I rode what he called 15 miles to Paralana, but over such rough country that it tried the horses more than three times the distance would have done on a good road. About half the journey was along the rocky bed of a creek, which, without such a guide as I had, I should have deemed in many places impassable for any but animals of the feline tribe. If I were to give a correct description of the route, I fear I should scarcely be believed; indeed, I feel almost incredulous myself now, when I read over the notes which I made just after that terrible ride. The first four or five miles were simply rough and uncomfortable for the horses, without being actually perilous; the " road" consisting of boulders and angular masses of stone in the creek, with an occasional variation of an ascent and descent over a spur of the range, perhaps 100 feet in height, and having a gradient of not less than 2 in 2, or, in other words, an angle of about 45 degrees. By way of further variety, these gentle ascents were sometimes covered with large stones, lying on a deep bed of loose sand, so that the horses' feet sunk between the stones, or sent them rolling down the hill behind. After little more than an hour's pleasant riding of this kind, we stopped at the foot of a tremendous hill, I should think 350 feet in height, at an angle of about 60 degrees from the horizon, and covered with loose stones in the way I have described. Mr. Frost told me there was a Mine on the other side, and when he discovered it he brought his horse over the hill, and down to the place where we stood! and to confirm what he said, as we ascended, he showed me the animal's tracks; however, we tied our horses to a tree in the gully to let them rest, and commenced the ascent on foot, but soon

"The foot was fain
Assistance from the hand to gain,"

and sometimes the stones rolling away from our tread, compelled us to go on all fours, or caused us, like the Irish boy going to school, to slide two yards back for one step forward. At last we reached the top, and were rewarded for our toil by the sight of similar ranges, almost as far as we could see, and a distant glimpse of the eastern plain through a gap in the mountains. Beneath our feet

The Pindilpena Mine,

On section 1538, lies about 150 feet from the top of this range, on the other side, and on a secondary hill parallel with the main range, and connected with it by a kind of solid bridge or causeway. I did not much relish the idea of descending and having to ascend again; but it must be done, so down we went, and found the usual ironstone rocks impregnated with Copper, both green carbonate and grey ore; the lode running nearly East and West for 70 or 88 yards, and varying in width, on the surface, from two to six feet. The geological appearance of the ground is singular, the following substances being all found within a few rods: ironstone, granite rock, greenstone, disintegrated quartz rock, felspar, limestone, micaceous schist, and some beautiful small crystals of quartz.

I should state that, notwithstanding the rough road we had travelled to reach this place, it is easily accessible in another direction, so that if the Mine were worked a tolerable road could be made to it.

———

Returning to our horses we found the descent, after having climbed to the top of the range from the Mine, even more difficult than the ascent, as we tried a new path, and not being able to see far before us were stopped twice by jutting and precipitous rocks; however, we reached the bottom in safety, and proceeded through what proved a far worse road than that we had left behind us. The recent rains had filled the creek; and its bed consisting in many places of large masses of smooth rock lying at an angle under the water, the horses found some difficulty in keeping their footing. Sometimes the water was up to the saddle girths, and in one place, where the only possibility of getting along was by going for about 50 yards in the bed of the creek, the water gradually deepened, and I continued to raise my feet until they were straight along the horse's back; I then experienced a peculiar sensation, which having felt before, I knew again; my horse was swimming; it was impossible to keep my feet dry, so I held on until we reached the shallow beyond. This part of the creek was entered through a narrow gap, between two huge rocks between 20 and 30 feet high, and over which we could scarcely have climbed ourselves, much less could we have taken our horses. In other parts of the creek our horses had to climb like cats over masses of rock, stepping up at once nearly four feet from the ground, and after going over a few yards of uncertain footing they sometimes had to jump down three or four feet into the creek. Occasionally, we dismounted and led them, and in one or two places the rocks were so extremely rough that we drove the horses before us, and clambered after them ourselves. Towards evening we reached Paralana, the station of John Jacob, Esq. Mr. Jacob had gone to Adelaide, and Mr. Comyn, the Overseer, was out at the time with Mr. Howitt, who was conveying the bones of Burke and Wills, the lost explorers, to Melbourne, viá Adelaide. Mrs. Comyn received us kindly, and set before us a sumptuous repast; comprising, amongst other delicacies, milk, fresh butter, and cake, and having been living for several days on rough bush fare, without any such dainties, we fully appreciated them. After drying our boots and stockings, resting our horses, and fastening on their shoes, which had become loose through their rough journey, we proceeded about five miles further in order to find better grass for the horses, and to shorten our march on the following day. Mrs. Comyn kindly gave us a bottle of milk (which lasted us for supper, and breakfast, and dinner the next day); besides supplying us with bread, butter, meat, tea, and sugar, so that we were unusually well off. I may mention, that about a mile and a half from Mr. Jacob's station there is a hot spring; but I did not visit it, being informed that the recent floods would have so overpowered it as to render it difficult to find. We camped about 9 p.m., on the edge of the Eastern Plain, having had a good road from the station, and a fine moonlight evening for our ride. We enjoyed a pot of tea, "au lait," and having made up luxurious couches of twigs of the tea tree, resigned ourselves to rural repose, lulled by the occasional notes of the birds, the distant tinkling of our horses' bells, and the musical hum of the mosquitoes. The next morning we were up at peep of day, and rose with that feeling of refreshment known only to those who can enjoy sleeping in the pure open air of a fine dry climate like ours. After breakfast we walked about half a mile to examine a claim (No. 1467) belonging to the Northern Mineral Association, and called by them "Wheal Susan;" this section is on low hills very little elevated above the plain, but divided by a gully below the level of the plain. There is a strong lode of ironstone running above the surface for 50 or 60 yards, and containing grey Copper Ore and green carbonate; there is also a good crosscourse running into the lode. There is a quantity of what I believe to be the old red sandstone on this section and in the neighbourhood, and as it is accompanied by mountain limestone, it may be considered as a very favorable indication of the proximity of coal. I therefore advised the proprietors of this claim to take measures for testing the ground by boring. I believe if two or three boring machines were introduced into the colony, capable of penetrating to a considerable depth, and worked by persons of enterprise and capital, such persons would be well repaid, and the ultimate results to the colony would be very beneficial. Gold is known to exist in many places, and coal has been found, at least a lignite, that would answer the purpose of house fuel very well; several other minerals of great value have been met with occasionally, and might be found in large quantities if a thorough and systematic search were made for them. But if no further good resulted from the introduction of boring machines, I believe that the benefit to be derived from a good supply of pure water would repay both the borers and those who employed them. The existence of coal is strongly suspected in several localities, and specimens of lignite, bituminous shale, &c., are sometimes met with. It is found in the neighbouring colonies, and I firmly believe that before long it will be in South Australia. I am of opinion, in common with many others, that half of our mineral wealth is not yet known, and the argument so often adduced is a very shallow and illogical one—that because a certain discovery has not been made for the six-and-twenty years of the colony's existence, therefore it never will be. I shall have occasion to touch upon this subject again by and bye, in referring to some important discoveries which have been recently made.

After examining the Wheal Susan, we saddled our horses and proceeded through another portion of the same creek we traversed yesterday, or rather through the Arcaroola (or Ahanola) Creek of which the Paralana is a tributary. Some of the scenery here is very grand, the sides of the creek, in many places, being composed entirely of rocks rising to a height of 300 to 400 feet, sometimes smooth and regular, and at others rugged and wild in their transposition. Occasionally we came upon a piece of less sterile country, some of the flats being covered with grass, and the sides of the hills with pines and scrub, amongst which were many beautiful flowering shrubs, the most conspicuous being a tall handsome shrub, bearing an elegant little blue flower with fringed edges ; and it is a curious fact that a dwarf plant only a

few inches high, and with totally different leaves, bears a flower
precisely similar to the other.

In the course of a couple of hours or so we arrived at

The Welcome Mines.

SECTION 1512 contains two or three lodes. A fine strong lode
runs nearly North and South, shewing for 50 or 60 yards on the
surface, four or five feet in width, and underlying to the West
about 18 inches in the fathom. The lode consists of steel grey
oxide, mixed with a greenish grey Ore; as the lode goes down it
appears very regular, and above two feet in width of solid ore,
yielding between 40 and 50 per cent. of Copper. The lode here
had been stoped away and about 25 tons were raised, dressed,
and bagged by two men in about six weeks. Another lode
was opened lower down the hill, and on the south end of the
section there are several veins of rich grey ore, ranging in width
from one to six inches, regular in their course and underlay, and
leading in the direction of the main lode. The country on this
Mine and about the neighbourhood consists of soft whitish killas
and a peculiar shaly kind of sandstone beautifully watermarked.
A good road has been cut from these Mines on to the Eastern
Plains, whence the route to Port Augusta is easy. The country
here is thickly timbered with mallee and mulga scrub, and gum
trees in the creeks. I also saw the native orange tree, very
similar in its general appearance to the true orange, but without
fruit, this not being the season.

Another Mine adjacent to the Welcome, and belonging to the
same Association, is called the Wheal Hancock after one of the
shareholders. This Mine is on section 1511 and 1537. The former
contains a good and distinct lode, traceable for about 250 yards, the
ore is about 18 inches wide and consists of fine grey oxide. There are
also some veins of good Ore in other places, and stains of Ore with
small pieces of malachite scattered on the surface near the lode,
which runs North-east and South-west, underlying westwards
into the hill. On the east of the lode there is a good cross-course
nearly at right angles with it, and containing beautiful " silver
grey Ore," as the miners here call it. On 1537 the Ore runs
almost the whole length of the claim, the lode outcropping for a
short distance and shewing solid grey Ore nearly two feet wide.
A little more than a mile from these sections we came to some
belonging to the proprietors of

The Ooroolbana Mine,

AND on one of which this Mine is situated. I thought as I rode
over one of these sections, that the country looked very favorable
for Copper, although there was no lode to be seen nor any special

indication. The Mine itself, if such it can be called, is on another section, and consists of an immense mass of rocks about 100 feet wide, and from 12 to 15 feet high, and which, I suppose, is called the lode. These are very hard quartzose rocks, and contain numerous green stains of Copper, but no Ore is found beneath the stains; a little further up the rise on which this reef is found some work has been done; the rocks have been broken, and some very fine thin veins of rich grey Ore exposed to view; but the depth of the workings does not exceed five feet. I was informed that 15 cwt. of Ore was raised here; if this be the case I am surprised that so much was obtained, and it must be taken as a proof of the richness of the Mine; but my opinion is that if it had been silver instead of Copper it would not have more than repaid the cost of raising it.

The Parabarana Mine

Is situated about 25 miles nearly north of Mr. Jacob's station, Paralana. I did not see the Mine, but have been favored with the following account of it, compiled from the Captain's report to the proprietors. I have reason to believe that the account may be depended on, and I have seen some fine specimens of Ore from the Mine. The country consists of clay-slate, and light soft sandstone. There are three distinct lodes on the section, two running North and South, and the other East and West; the latter is visible on the surface for about 250 yards, going over a small hill about 50 feet in height, it then crosses a gully on to the next hill. The small hill contains a large quantity of Ore and Copper stains; the lode is very wide, and a cross-cut has been driven under the hill and across the lode, for a length of 15 fathoms from the gully level; the lode has an underlay to the South of about 18 inches in the fathom. Two pits have also been sunk on the lode—one in the creek, and the other at a short distance from it—and in each of these places the lode improves as it goes down, the stains of Ore giving place to green and blue carbonate. The other lode, to the East of that just described, is traceable about 150 yards on the surface; in some parts it crops out of the ground, and in one place it is estimated that 100 tons of the lode are visible above the surface. It has been opened on in two places, and its width has been ascertained to be four feet, consisting of red and grey oxide, intermixed with spar and a little iron. The third lode is three and a half feet in width, and underlies about three feet in the fathom. A shaft has been sunk five fathoms in this lode through malachite and green carbonate of 35 or 40 per cent. produce, intermixed with prian and gossan. Several smaller lodes are also found on the section, containing

good Ore. There is a good supply of wood within five miles of
the section, and plenty of water close to the Mine. This is the
most distant Mine (North) with which I am acquainted. The
road which would be used for carting away the Ore lies, for some
distance, along the Eastern Plains, and, I suppose, the distance
from Port Augusta is above 270 miles.

The Sir Dominick and Daly Mines.

I NOW proceed to describe this very rich batch of mineral sections,
the property of the Northern Mineral Association, and commencing about four miles North of the Yudanamutana sections.
Nearly the whole of the ground between these two points is
metalliferous, in a greater or less degree.

The Daly Mine (claim 1464) is situated on a steep hill nearly
200 feet in height, and consisting of soft whitish country,
apparently a kind of pipeclay or fireclay. There is a reef of
quartzoze rocks running East and West, near the top of the hill,
and forming, apparently, the back of a lode, which, however, has
not been opened up in such a way as to shew its regular course.
Stoping has been done to some extent at the side of the hill, and
about 100 feet from the gully, and has laid bare a large quantity
of fine Ore, chiefly grey oxide, in strong veins running down into
the hill; some of these veins open out to a considerable size, so
much so that large blocks of Ore are obtained. I saw one very
fine mass of solid grey oxide, and which would weigh, I should
think, fully three tons, and average, throughout, 50 per cent. of
Copper. Some fine specimens of red oxide and green and blue
carbonates are also found here. Several other blocks weighing
some hundredweights each were also at grass. To give an idea
of the easy nature of the ground, I may state that a drive was
carried 15 fathoms into the hill, at 35s. per fathom, and although
its position and direction were not selected so judiciously as
might have been the case, veins of Ore were continually met with
in cutting it. The workings being on the side of a steep hill, the
Ore as turned out is for the most part sent rolling down to the
bottom, where it is dressed and bagged. Nearly 90 tons of Ore,
averaging 40 per cent produce, were raised at this Mine by four
men, in little more than three months, or perhaps it would be
correct to say in three months, as some time was occupied in
cutting, blasting, and clearing a road through a rocky gully to
some of the sections. Higher up the hill, and towards the
South-Eastern part of the section, there is a quantity of stones
of Ore scattered over the surface, and indications of other lodes.
I picked up some fine large crystals of quartz in this place.

"Old Noll's Mine," on section 1482, adjoins the former at the
South-West corner. It is on a hill of considerable elevation, and

contains a fine deposit of green carbonate and red and grey oxide of Copper in a large reef of rocks running for some distance on the top of the range. In many places, were there is no appearance of Ore, the breaking of what seems to be nothing but common quartzose rock discloses rich specimens of Copper, and there appears to be a large quantity on this section, Indeed, many tons could be *quarried* out with the pick and crowbar.

The "Sir Dominick" Mine is very similar in appearance to the preceding, and lies to the east of that section. The lode, which is from eight to ten feet in width, contains red and grey oxide, and green carbonate of Copper in considerable quantities; it is visible on the surface for nearly half a mile in length. The reef of rocks, forming the back of the lode on the summit of the hill, is very bold, and in some places the path, if such it can be called, is so narrow as to be perilous to an unsteady foot; a strong puff of wind from either side might send a weak or nervous man rolling 300 feet down into the gully. I was reminded here of Sir Walter Scott's descriptions of Highland scenery :—

"The loose crags whose threatening mass
Lay tottering o'er the hollow pass,
As if an infant's touch could urge
Their headlong passage down the verge."

Many of the surrounding hills are similar in their appearance, and the view from the Sir Dominick is extensive and beautiful. No work has been done on either this or "Old Noll's Mine."

The Stanley Mine, on section 1465, is in a kind of basin, and in lower and more settled country than the three Mines I have just described. A short distance to the North rises the bold range called Freeling Heights, the Yudanamutana ranges bound it on the East, while hills of more moderate elevation rise on the South and West. There is a magnificent main lode running East and West through this section for about half a mile, and proved to contain fine Ore for nearly 400 yards, and probably for a much greater distance. The prevailing Ore is grey oxide, there are also blue and green carbonates and some malachite. The back of the lode consists chiefly of fine gossan and ironstone. A branch lode from the South-east runs into the main lode, and contains a large percentage of Bismuth in combination with the Copper. When I examined this Mine it had not been opened, but, after a careful inspection, I expressed an opinion that it would, when worked, prove to be an exceedingly valuable property. Since I saw it the lode has been opened in two or three places, and with most satisfactory results.

Another section (No. 1553) which I visited, and belonging to the same company, is near to the Yudanamutana Mines; the discoverers named it the Daisy Mine. It contains two lodes, one of which is about four feet wide, and traceable for 80 yards along the surface, carrying grey and red oxide and green carbonate in fine gossan. There are also limestone and quartz on the section. The same proprietary have several other claims which promise to be quite worth working, but which it is needless to notice separately. There is, however, another claim belonging to a portion of the same owners, and named after the discoverer,

The Wheal Frost.

THIS contains so extraordinary a deposit of Copper Ore, as to demand a special notice. It is on a range about 350 feet high from a creek on one side, and between 400 and 500 feet from a creek on the other side. It is about two miles from the Daly and four from the Yudanamutana Mines. The top of the range, for 80 or 90 feet in height, consists of a mass of granitic rock, from which the upper soil has either slipped or been washed away, leaving the rock exposed. It is almost perpendicular and contains numerous green stains of Copper, visible for a distance of a quarter of a mile or more. I and my guide climbed up the face of this rock for a height of 60 or 70 feet, by means of small holes and inequalities in its surface, and almost everywhere, even where there were no stains to be seen, we found rich Copper Ore—grey oxide and green carbonate; especially in small caves or holes in the rock. Below these bare rocks, and down to the gully, we found a quantity of stones of Ore scattered over the surface; amongst them were bits of malachite and various oxides and carbonates. Ironstone, gossan, killas, limestone, sandstone, and greenstone, are found here. If the surface indications form a criterion of what may be found in depth, a very large deposit of Copper should be met with on this claim.

The same proprietors have another claim (No. 1668), called "Wheal Maria," between the Daly and Yudanamutana Mines. It is a very fair section, and has a good lode of Ore traceable for 130 yards North and South, in a favorable country for Copper.

The natives in the North, although brought more recently into contact with Europeans than those in the older settled districts of the colony, fully understand the mysterious power possessed by the whites of making paper speak, and a blackfellow, if sent on a message, likes to carry a written paper with him, as a kind of warrant or authority for his errand. They soon observed me "taking notes" and making sketches, and at once dubbed me "Paper Masser." Gentlemen connected with the Mines, by the same rule, they call "Copper Massers." The Captains of the Mines are thus designated, but if anyone appears to possess authority over the Captains, like Mr. Martin, the Superintendent of the Yudanamutana Mines, for instance, they call him "Big One Copper Masser," and this without reference to the relative stature of the individuals in question. I have in my note book a number of interesting memoranda about the natives; but having been unavoidably delayed in the preparation of this work, I fear I must postpone the writing up of that information for some future opportunity, and proceed with my description of the Mines. I will, however, allude to the existence of a tradition pretty general amongst the blacks, throughout the colony, respecting a huge animal called by some a Bunyip, and which they say "plenty eat up blackfellow." I have myself conversed with blacks who professed to have seen this dreadful creature, and to have ineffectually given it battle, as they said it would break their spears with its teeth. This tradition is very well known in the colonies, and I mention it here simply to state that it exists also amongst the natives of the Far North; and to offer the suggestion, whether the fossil bones discovered at Herr Got Springs, near Mount Attraction, belong to the animal referred to.

Before starting on my return trip, I may refer to a few of the physical features of a portion of the country, beyond the most northerly point which I visited, and which have been described to me by Mr. A. P. Burtt, who has travelled through that country. The ranges beyond the Freeling heights gradually diminish in elevation, and are more disconnected than those farther south; and in what is called Stuart's country, most of his "Mounts" are low hills, many of them not more than 50 feet in height. Several of these mounts have fine springs on their summits; the "Blanche Cup," named after Lady MacDonnell, our late Governor's Lady, is a beautiful example; here there is a spring of delicious water on the top of a hillock, and in a kind of crater, or cup about 30 feet in diameter, and of a considerable depth. The country beyond 400 miles North of Adelaide is more level and "broken" than it is further south. There are belts of scrub and patches of good country, here and there long tracts without water, and then fine springs and creeks containing fish; salt water lakes and fresh water lakes; springs impregnated with soda, some having a peculiar smell, as that at Petamora, and the Welcome Spring; this odour, which resembles that of gunpowder, goes off after the water has been exposed for some time to the air, and does not appear to rise from any deleterious quality in the water, which is said to be soft and also perfectly sweet when used for making tea and bread. The Petamora Spring bubbles up with some force to a height of several inches above the surface. Timber, generally, is very scarce in the North, large trees being seldom found except in watercourses.

While in the neighbourhood of the Daly Mines, I heard a curious noise made by a bird, and closely resembling the sound caused by pouring liquor out of a bottle. Another bird which I have also heard elsewhere produced a sound like the tinkling of a large cattle bell. The lyre bird and, I am told, a variety of the bird of Paradise are also met with in some parts of this country; but as I have only seen or heard of two places in the North at all Paradisaical in their character, I should conclude, if the latter bird is found elsewhere, it must either have lost itself or been expelled from its native bowers.

In riding from the Welcome Mines towards Illinawurtina we passed through a fine valley bearing the rather ostentatious name of the Vale of Avoca. The scenery is certainly very fine ; the ranges on either side rise to a height of from 400 to 600 feet, that to the North being higher and bolder than the other. At the top of the range, immense bare rocks, like those previously described at Wheal Frost, rise here and there in fantastic shapes, and then smooth and flatlike flagstones, while below, where there is some soil and the slope is more gentle, grass, scrub, pines, and pretty flowering shrubs, grow from the foot of these rocks down into the gully. On the other side the hill is less bold and remarkable. I suppose in the case of the first range the soil has been washed away from the top, as seems to have been frequently the case in the North, leaving the rocks exposed. Below the large masses of rock, and at the distance of a few yards, an irregular wall of rocks, ranging from ten to more than twenty feet in height, runs for a considerable length. There are several apertures in this wall, one of which is remarkable from the regularity of its shape, and from the fact of its being spanned by a natural bridge, composed of a single stone 15 or 20 feet long, and as regularly formed as if dressed and erected by masons. It happens, singularly enough, that a pine has fallen over the bridge, and its dead trunk looks like a hand-rail placed there for the convenience of passengers. After coming through the Vale of Avoca we entered the Arcaroola or Illinawurtina Creek, one of the finest I saw in the North, and containing a large quantity of fine gum timber and good water. The Illinawurtina run contains a considerable extent of excellent country, where genuine *grass* grows luxuriantly after rain. Here I saw the Nardoo plant, to which such a sad interest is attached from the fact of its having supplied the unfortunate explorers, Burke and Wills, with a scanty subsistence for some time after their return to Cooper's Creek. The taste of the seed is far from pleasant, and it produces a slight burning sensation in the throat ; I must be very hard pressed indeed before I should resort to it as an article of food.

On leaving Illinawurtina, where I spent two days very pleasantly with Mr. H. Hughes, Mr. Scott's overseer, I started, in company with Mr. Burtt, and made for the Western Plain. The country through which we travelled was undulating and pretty well grassed. About four miles South from Illinawurtina, we saw Benbonyàta (pronounced Benbone-yàta), " survey point Z," the highest land in South Australia. I cannot ascertain the exact height, as the calculations have never been worked out, but it is considered to be more than 4,000 feet above the level of the sea. This is a bold massive-looking range, several miles in length, running nearly North-east and South-west, between Gammon Hill and Mount McKinlay.

After riding 12 or 14 miles we came into country exhibiting peculiar geological formation ; clay-slate rocks rise out of the ground in every direction like gravestones in an old churchyard.

There are numerous low hills, some of them rising rather abruptly, one in particular, called Fortress Hill, is a mount about 200 feet in height, and having a rocky summit on which the stones are deposited with almost the regularity of mason's work, giving it the appearance of a fortification. Its diameter at the top is, perhaps, 120 or 130 feet, and at the base about 300 or 350 feet. Beneath this cap of rock the sides of the hill are covered with scrub and small loose stones, but no other large rocks are to be seen.

A little beyond Fortress Hill we reached Mr. Thomas Gill's station, in the midst of the "grave stone country." Proceeding westward, we came upon the Frome river, which, when I saw it, really appeared to deserve the name, though it is frequently dry for the greater part of its course. I came upon the Frome at a point near to a magnificent pool, called by the natives " Murry-wyanna ;" it was then a fine sheet of water from 30 to 40 yards wide, above 150 yards long, and about 20 feet deep at its greatest depth. Rocks rise perpendicularly on the side of the creek, next the deepest part, and I believe that the water here has never been known to fail in the dryest season. Having supped at Mr. Gill's station, we rode about seven miles beyond to camp, in order to find good feed for our horses, and in this we were very fortunate. The next morning we were up by daybreak, and " making tracks" for

The Mount Lyndhurst Mine,

On the edge of the Western Plain. This Mine has received its name from Mount Lyndhurst, although that hill is nearly ten miles distant; but I believe it is the nearest trigonometrical station of any importance. The Mine is on low hilly ground, no part of which I should consider more than 100 feet high. Nevertheless, the view across the plain is very extensive, and many far-distant hills, both amongst the ranges and on the edge of the plain, are distinctly to be seen.

The geological formation of the ground consists of clayslate, micaceous schist, limestone, and quartz. The poorest indications are found on the highest part of the ground, where the quartz predominates, but there is a lode traceable on the surface for about 130 yards, and from two to three feet wide, carrying strong stains of Copper and some good stones of Ore. The back of the lode, as usual, is composed of ironstone and gossan. This lode has been opened in two or three places, and some green carbonate and grey oxide raised. About 200 yards further East, another lode is met with, and a shaft has been sunk four fathoms on the lode, which underlies about 18 inches in the fathom, and looks very well indeed ; it is nearly four feet wide, containing grey and red oxides ; some native or malleable Copper was also found here. A good cross-course runs into this lode from the North-East. There is another lode running nearly East and West, and traceable about 70 yards on the surface. The back of this lode consists of ironstone and gossan, strongly impregnated with Copper. The lode underlies from two to two and a half feet in the fathom, towards the North, and contains malachite, greenish grey Ore, and liver-colored Ore; it is from 18 inches to two feet wide.

A fourth lode is found about 50 yards from the preceding, and running parallel with it; the solid Ore in this lode is 15 inches wide; it contains similar Ore to that last mentioned, and fine yellow Ore in addition. At another part of the section there is a considerable surface deposit of Ore scattered over several rods of ground, and containing green carbonate, malachite, and grey Ores, varying in value from 20 to above 40 per cent. of Copper.

This Mine, being on the edge of the Western Plain, is very favorably situated with respect to the line which will most likely be taken for the formation of a tramway.

––––––––––

It was my intention after visiting the Mount Lyndhurst Mine, to proceed to Mount Coffin to inspect the "New Burra Burra," but to my great regret circumstances arose which prevented my doing so, and I was obliged to strike through the hills to Mount Rose, and thence to Owieandana, where we passed the night. We here met with Mr. H. C. Gleeson who was returning from the Daly and Welcome Mines, in which he is interested. The next morning our horses were missing, and after three hours of weary wandering over the hills, they were found about five miles away on the road back. We thus made a rather late start, but were determined on reaching Angipena before dark, and this we accomplished, without pushing our horses beyond the ordinary pace for bush travelling—five miles an hour. Although only a fortnight had elapsed since the rain commenced, its effects were very manifest in the growth of the grass, and the freshened appearance of vegetation generally. Many parts of our route, to-day, were really beautiful; grassy slopes, with thinly scattered gums and pines, occasionally diversified with thick belts of mallee scrub, or bold rocky hills, and every now and again a fine "gum creek," with abundance of water in pools. The Frome, especially, is one of the finest creeks in the North, and contains some good timber. The Mudlipena Gap, through which this creek runs, is a fine piece of rocky scenery, and would be extremely grand and imposing if the walls were a hundred feet higher; they are only about 100 feet in height but extend for a considerable length, at least on one side, while the other side, except in the narrowest part of the gap, is less wild and rocky in appearance. A pretty little gravelly flat of four or five acres, is enclosed between the hills close to the gap and the road then takes a sudden bend to the left, revealing some fine pools of water. As we rode along, when within about eight miles of Angipena, a turn in the road displayed to my astonished gaze what appeared like a line of telegraph posts ; but on ascending a rising ground, I saw that these posts encircled a large space of undulating conntry, having on one side a rough erection of wood, called the Grand Stand, behind which was an immense number of broken bottles, the *debris* of former " meetings ;" at intervals round the circle were short pieces of fencing, designated by the name of hurdles : in fact we had come upon the Angipena race-course, the only one, I believe, North of Mount Remarkable, and to it, I am told, visitors have been known to come a distance ot about 200 miles! The number present last year was about 50 ; a good muster, considering the very scattered nature of the population. I understand a large amount of cash changed hands on the occasion, for bushmen are fond of sport, and generally very free with their money. The company all camped at night on the ground, many of them being too far overcome to travel, and, had it been otherwise, they would have been unable to find accommodation. The country, as we neared Angipena, was very pretty, indeed I could have fancied myself in the neighbourhood of Mount Barker ; the land was well grassed, and trees were much more plentiful than in most parts of the North.

Angipena is the most distant police-station in the North, and four troopers reside there. They have, occasionally, long and important journeys to perform ; for instance, Corporal Wauchop was ordered to convey despatches from the Committee of the Victorian Expedition to Mr. Howitt, at Cooper's Creek. This he accomplished in 21 days from Adelaide, the distance travelled being nearly 800 miles, a considerable part of the way through very rough, inhospitable country.

Angipena station is in a pretty dell, thickly wooded with pines, and a few gums, and surrounded by steep, but not very high hills. About half a mile East from the trig a mineral discovery has been made, and a claim taken out, which has been named, after one of the proprietors,

The Wheal Besley.

THE indications and nature of the country here are very favorable ; there are two lodes on the section, bearing very good gossan impregnated with green and blue carbonates and containing occasional good stones of Ore. The lodes run North and South, and are traceable across the section for a distance of about 300 yards. Besides the green and blue carbonates, there is liver-colored and yellow Ore, scattered in places on the surface.

About two miles eastwards from Angipena is the once celebrated

H

Mochatoona Mine.

THIS was at one time believed to be such a wonderful discovery that many miners left the Burra, hoping to find more remunerative employment here, though the Mochatoona is 300 miles beyond the Burra. For a short time a number were employed; but there appears to have been, by all accounts, some little mismanagement, for although several tons of Ore were raised, the ground does not appear to have been judiciously worked, and the funds of the proprietors were exhausted before the Mine was fairly tested. The ground looks very favorable for mining, and it may be that some future adventurers, having more money, more enterprise, or more skill than the first, will yet develop a valuable property here.

Before leaving Angipena, I saw a native's grave. A semicircle of stones, about five feet in diameter, and only a few inches high, was placed at the head and covered with branches like a native's "wurley" or hut; two or three large stones were placed over the head of the body, and a fire was kept burning for several days on the ground at the feet. The ground was bare of grass, and was swept regularly for some time after the burial. The mourners at the funeral walked in procession round the grave, and each threw a large stone, with considerable force, against an adjacent tree, so as to make a permanent mark in it. I have described this grave, and the ceremonies connected with it, because they differ materially from those practised in other parts of the country. It is pretty well known that some of the natives place their dead on a stage, raised like a high bed on four sticks, and the body dries in the sun. Others deposit the corpse in some hollow tree, and others bury their dead, but without the care and ceremonies described above.

From Angipena we proceeded to Nuccaleena, and on our way visited

The Wirryoota Mine.

IT is situated amongst low hills, or rather undulating ground, to the westward of a main range, running nearly North and South, about five miles from Mount Stuart, and near the Wirryoota creek. There is a well-defined lode running lengthwise through the section, and having, as usual, a back of ironstone; the surrounding country being killas and quartz. A few stains of Copper are found here and there on the surface, and two or three holes, five or six feet in depth, have been sunk on the lode. At these places the lode has good walls, and seems going down almost perpendicularly, and from one to two feet wide, carrying good stones of grey ore and green carbonate.

We had previously taken a look at the Mount Stuart Mine; but I refer to that below, in order to bring consecutively under notice, all the Mines of the Great Northern Mining Company.

The Mount Stuart Mine,

Is at present not being worked. A large mass of rocks appears to have crossed a gully and been cut through by the force of water, or by some other effort of nature. They contained stains of Copper and a good vein of Ore. Two shafts were sunk near the rocks, one on each side the gully, and there was some Ore on the floors, blue and green carbonates, but the general appearances were not favorable. One of these shafts was sunk 10 fathoms, and a drive was then carried 10 fathoms, but without cutting the lode.

Proceeding onwards we came to a station of Messrs. Chambers and Finke's, called Bobmoonie West, and here we found a fine spring of water and good country; from near this place we had a fine view of Mount Deception, and a large extent of hilly country on this side of it.

Nuccaleena.

On leaving the Wirryoota we had a pleasant ride of ten or twelve miles to Nuccaleena, where we arrived about 8 p m. This Mine had an immense surface deposit of rich Ore, on the side of a hill, from which above 600 tons were taken. The lode was then lost, and the water stopped further progress, until the engine was erected. After the water was in fork (all pumped out) the lode was recovered at the 10-fathom level, and when I visited the Mine it presented a most encouraging appearance. The lode was proved for 18 fathoms in length, with well-defined walls, and underlying 18 inches in the fathom; the width of the Ore (black oxide and sulphurets) being from five to seven feet. A winze was sunk three fathoms five feet on the lode, and from it seven tons of good Ore were raised, the quality improving with the depth.

The engine-shaft is 18 fathoms in depth, having been commenced about 12 fathoms above the level of the creek, in the side of the hill. The stopes are 33 fathoms North of East, from the engine-shaft, and five levels have been driven on the course of the lode, all the "backs" and "bottoms" being stoped away. An adit was driven into the hill, and cut the lode in nine fathoms, and which was then driven on for 40 fathoms, a large amount of stoping being done. At the 10-fathom level a winze is sunk, about 15 fathoms East of the whim shaft, leaving that extent of ground which carries the lode recently recovered. The main cross-cut was driven 22 fathoms South into the hill to cut the lode, but was temporarily stopped. If it prove successful, it will give the stope of all the hill, and enable a tramway to be laid to convey the Ore to the floors. The Mine is under the superintendence of Captain Pearson Morrison, a gentleman of considerable experience both in Cornwall and America.

This Mine presents a more pleasing appearance, as to its buildings, and all the arrangements at "grass," than any Mine in the North; there is an air of comfort as well as of business about the place, which its more recent competitors have not yet attained to. Moreover, the 16-inch cylinder steam-engine adds very much to the appearance of the Mine. This, which is a low-pressure condensing engine, was made by Mr. G. Wyatt, of Adelaide, for the Reedy Creek Mine; it was then used, for a time, at the Charlton Mine, and at last found its way here, being the first engine erected in the Far North. The Captain's apartments, office, and three other buildings of stone, are erected on a terrace opposite the engine, and present a frontage of nearly 100 feet. There are, also, substantial stone stables, a good store, smith's shop, workshop, &c., besides a general store, established for the purpose of supplying the wants of the miners; also a doctor's house, and about 20 good pine huts for the men.

A Mechanic's Institute has been formed here, and the men seem to devote themselves after work to useful study, or to innocent recreation. They have established a judge and jury club, for the trial of petty offences amongst themselves, and it has been found to work well. There is, also, a good musical band, including some good singers among its members, the instrumental part consisting of a drum, triangle, "bones," violins, and a concertina. On the evening of my arrival the band was "discoursing sweet music," the sound of which, reverberating through the hills, was very enlivening, especially to weary travellers, who had been long absent from anything of the kind.

Another of the Company's properties, is

The Two Brothers.

It is situated about two miles nearly North of Nuccaleena, on a hill of some altitude. At first this Mine looked exceedingly promising, a lode of rich red oxide, two feet in width, being traceable the whole length of the section, but when they commenced sinking and driving the lode was lost. I can hardly conceive that a regular lode of this nature would be succeeded by nothing in depth, and I should hope that when a favorable opportunity presents itself, researches will be resumed in this quarter.

The next of the Great Northern Company's Mines which I have to notice is

The Oratunga Mine.

It is situated about seven miles South-east of Nucaleena amidst low hilly country. There is a good lode averaging about 12 feet in width and containing very fair Ore. Shafts have been sunk on the lode, varying in depth from 6 to 15 fathoms, and Ore was obtained in each, nearly 100 tons being raised. At a depth of about 12 or 13 fathoms a peculiar slide seemed to have taken place in the lode and a floor came in having a slope of about 25 °. This was followed down until the miners were stopped by water. In another place, about 20 tons of 30 per cent. Ore were raised from a counter of the lode, and a shaft sunk with the view of cutting the lode at 18 or 20 fathoms in depth but here the water stopped proceedings. It is intended to erect a donkey engine which is expected to be sufficient for keeping the water in fork for the present; and operations will then be resumed. The Mine is considered a very promising one.

Another of these Mines is called

The Mooroo Mine,

On the edge of the Eastern Plain. The first indications were found here on a hill about 130 feet in height, and which was stained with Copper from top to bottom. Two shafts were sunk to the depths of six and eight fathoms respectively, and about 20 tons of Ore was raised, but the water coming in rather strongly, and no regular and promising lode having been met with, the work was put a stop to.

Nevertheless there are strong indications of mineral existing in the neighbourhood, and several sections, on which Ore was found scattered over the surface, were explored, but without any particular results.

This Mine is a few miles to the West of Prism Hill, one of the trigonometrical stations, and about twenty-five miles North of Mount Chambers, which is about six miles to the North of

The Mount Chambers Mine,

WHICH is in low country, a little to the South of the hill so-
called, near the Eastern Plain, and is situated between hills of
moderate elevation.   The surface of the ground is covered with
boulders of primitive limestone.   Several large blocks of
malachite were found in a clear space, about 20 feet wide,
running North and South between the boulders.   There is
no regularly defined lode, although in one place the arrangement
of the Ore bore very much the appearance of one.   Blocks of
Ore were obtained in three different parts of the section, at
intervals of 120 or 130 yards.   The country being moderately
hard pipeclay, is easily worked, and requires no timbering.
Several shafts were sunk without finding a lode, although a good
deal of malachite and green carbonate is scattered on the surface.
The Ore is rich, some samples having assayed between 50 and 60
per cent.   Operations on this Mine are suspended for the
present.

Vesey's Claim.

No. 1630, about 10 or 12 miles North-East of Nuccaleena, and
on the Warrewena run, is a valuable property.   There is a well-
defined lode running nearly through the section, and containing
very rich Ore: green carbonate and grey oxide, some of the
latter containing about 70 per cent. of Copper.   The country
consists of clayslate and pipeclay.   Some little work has been
done, but the recent rains prevented my examining the pit that
had been sunk.

After leaving Nuccaleena, as we approached Moolooloo, the
hills beyond presented a most curious appearance, the jutting
rocks (indurated clay-slate, I believe) on the top and down the
sides, pursuing a tortuous course, and looking in the distance
like gigantic serpents crawling over the country.

That part of the country between Moolooloo and Angorigena
having been noticed in a former page, need not be again described.
From Angorigena I proceeded to

The Mallee Hut Claim,

No. 1621, belonging to Messrs. Finke & Kerfert.   This claim is
about six miles S. by. W. of Mount Emily, and though at present
nothing very extensive has been discovered, the indications are

decidedly good. A lode has been opened in a creek near the road
side, and shows good walls and favorable country, killas and
flucan with fine gossan in the lode, and a fair amount of green
carbonate of Copper and chocolate and yellow Ore. The lode is
nearly perpendicular, and about 18 inches wide; an adit was
driven into the hill on the course of the lode, and a small shaft
commenced at the mouth of the adit and in the creek, but after
being sunk about six feet the water came in and filled the hole.
Since the water has subsided, I am informed that two tons of
good Ore have been raised here. A short distance, only five or
six yards to the North, and about 20 or 25 yards to the West,
another lode has been opened close to the surface, unless it be a
heave of the same lode, but from the appearance of the country
I do not think it is. There was but little Ore visible here at the
time I saw the place, but the indications were good, and the lode
carried remarkably well-defined walls.

From this claim I crossed the hills to

𝔄roona,

THE "Garden of the North," a station belonging to Mr. Thomas
Phillips, and formerly to Mr. Hayward. Although I have no
Mine to describe here, I devote a special notice to this beautiful
locality, as I saw no other place in the North at all to be compared with it. Coming upon it after a weary day's ride, and just
as the rays of the setting sun were casting their golden beams
over the landscape, I thought it one of the loveliest spots I ever
beheld; and even after making every allowance for the enthu-
siasm of a first impression under the circumstances, a critical
study of the place must result in a judgment highly favorable to
its appearance. There is a combination of the wild and grand,
with what is softer and more gentle; and without any violent
contrast, which would mar the general effect. The scene is
perfectly harmonious; and if any improvement could be desired,
it is that hinted at by an enthusiastic Hibernian, when he first
saw the place, and exclaimed, " Sure its like Killarney, intirely,
barrin' the lake."

A fine, bold, massive range, terminating at the South in Hayward's Bluff, and 600 or 700 feet high from the valley, rises
majestically in the background. A space of about 100 feet
downwards from its summit consists of bare rock, of a reddish-
brown color, and, I presume, either granitic or indurated sandstone. Below the rock, innumerable steep spurs proceed from
the range; and these are covered with vegetation of various kinds.
Near the top there is little grass, but scrub and pines; lower
down the pines become thicker, and gum trees are interspersed
amongst them; until when the valley is reached, the trees become

more luxuriant in their growth, and numerous handsome shrubs, wild-flowers, and grasses, abound. Although our Hibernian friend missed the lake, Aroona is one of the most remarkable places for water in the colony. A low hill rises with a gentle slope in the centre of the valley, and is completely surrounded by a creek, in which, I believe, water is to be found throughout the year. About 60 feet above the creek there are numerous surface springs from which the water flows, and some of them are complete bogs, so as to require fencing to keep out the cattle ; the water being conveyed, in shoots, to troughs fixed on hard ground. A good garden is made below these springs, and can be irrigated *ad libitum;* it contains fine weeping willows, splendid vines and fig-trees, loaded with fruit—besides other fruit and ornamental trees—and vegetables that would grace any horticultural show. I measured cauliflowers, less than three months old, two feet six inches high, above the stalk, and the flowers nine inches in diameter! The house is built of large pines, placed upright, trimmed and fitted close together, and the supply of water is derived from one of the surface springs above mentioned and close to the door.

The creek, a branch of which forms a horseshoe turn in front of the house, runs through a beautiful grassy flat about a quarter of a mile wide, and joins the Brachina a mile lower down.

The best view of Aroona is obtained from the side of the hill to the East of the valley where some masses of rock and handsome trees add to the effect of the foreground. Looking Southwards from the same stand point, there is a fine view of a succession of curious hills, the most Northern side of each being steep and generally capped with rocks, while the South side is gently sloping. This is called the A B C range from an idea that the number of the separate hills is the same as the letters of the alphabet. There is a beautiful valley, well grassed, and containing some good timber on either side of the range. St. Mary's Peak, one of the highest points of the Wilpena Pound range, towers away in the distance. I think the 20 miles of country, including Aroona and Wilpena, contain more subjects for the artist's pencil than any other part in the North. Before concluding my notice of this favored spot, I may be permitted to add that the residents are well worthy of the place. I spent nearly two days most agreeably with Mr. Phillips and his family, from whom I met with great kindness. Even the animals here seemed more cheerful and lively than in most other places, the native pigeons were heard cooing around, and numerous little songsters twittered amongst the bushes. One pretty bird—the shepherd's companion—occupied a willow tree near the room where I slept, and kept up a pleasing kind of chirrup all through the night until daybreak. I honored him with the title of the South Australian Nightingale—just by way of encouraging his laudible attempts.

Before leaving Aroona, Mr. and Mrs. Phillips kindly accompanied me to see the Brachina, a creek somewhat like the Arcaroola or Ahanola farther North. Tremendous rocky ranges rise on either side to a height of 600 or 800 feet, forming, in some places, almost perpendicular walls for a considerable elevation; yet amongst these rocks, wherever a little soil was to be found, a tree or bush of some kind might be seen. The creek itself contained many fine trees and handsome shrubs, and large pools of water. This watercourse receives several tributaries, and at times, after a heavy thunderstorm, though miles distant, a torrent seven or eight feet deep will come rushing down with irresistible force and with the shortest possible notice.

From Aroona I rode to

Wilpena Pound.

THE country through which I passed was pleasant and the road good. The magnificent hills encircling the pound presented an object of which the eye did not soon weary. For the whole distance I scarcely lost sight of some portion of them. The most Northerly peak, and I believe the highest, is St. Mary's; the next, about four miles to the South-East, is Point Bonney; and the most Southerly, six miles further, is Rawnsley's Bluff. St. Mary's Peak is said to be 1,500 feet from the base to the summit. It presents a peculiar appearance, having a kind of frill or collar of rocks surrounding it, about 50 feet from the top. Many of the peaks in the North are similarly encircled, including others in the Pound ranges.

The approach to Mr. H. S. Price's station is up a broad flat, through which the Wilpena creek, or Pasmore river runs; this stream rises in the pound, and contains a never failing supply of excellent water. The appearance of this place rivals that of Aroona, probably some persons would prefer it, but each has beauties of its own. The scenery of Aroona is more wild and Highland-like, while that of Wilpena, near the station, is of a softer, more homely English beauty. The land is well timbered with fine pines and gums, and the clear flowing creek, with rushes growing on its banks, supplies an interesting and practically important feature in the scene. Mr. Price was in Adelaide at the time of my visit, but he had kindly given orders for my reception. It being shearing time every hand on the station was busily employed, and I was obliged to find my way into the Pound without a guide. This was not a very easy matter for a stranger, for the entrance is up a narrow gorge, the bottom of which, except a narrow path, consists of a complete bog or morass, covered with most luxuriant grass, for no cattle can venture on the treacherous soil to eat the tempting herbage. In some parts this path has been made more secure by placing stones at the edge of the bog. After riding above a mile, I came to a fence across the gorge at a place where it would be impossible

I

for cattle to climb the hills on either side. There were slip-rails on the path, so passing through I rode a little further until I was stopped by smooth sloping rocks, at such an angle that the horse could not pass over them; I therefore tied him to a tree, and with some little difficulty proceeded on foot. The upper rocks underlapped those below, and where they did so, in some instances, there were considerable pools of water. After a while I got fairly into the Pound, and the magnificent sight that met my gaze, would have repaid many a weary day's journey. A gently undulating, but nearly level surface, extending for 10 or 12 miles in length by nearly three in breadth, covered with luxuriant grass, and having noble pines and gum trees dotted about in clumps, as in an English park, and interspersed with shrubs and flowers. The giant hills which surround this wonderful natural pound frown darkly down on the enclosed plain, bidding defiance to the cattle to escape over their lofty and rugged summits. The sides of the hills are covered to a considerable height with shrubs and small trees, and higher up apparently with low scrub. Mr. Selwyn, the Government Geologist of Victoria, says of the Pound—"It's singularly grand and picturesque appearance far surpassed anything I had previously seen in Australia. * * * It is not a volcanic crater, nor in any way due to volcanic action, of which there is no trace in the neighbourhood, but simply to a sinclinal undulation of the upper sandstones, * * * the highest beds of the great anticlinal, and forming the summits of all the higher peaks from Mount Remarkable northwards."

From Wilpena, I rode the same evening to Arkaba, on the East side of Elder's Range, passing to the West of the Druid's and Chase's Ranges. On the road I encountered a thunder storm, and had a specimen of the way in which the country is suddenly flooded. The flats were almost entirely covered with water, and the creeks soon rose several feet, rushing along like torrents.

From Arkaba I rode to Kanyaka, intending to visit some mineral claims which I had missed seeing on my way up; but being seized with an attack of illness, I was unable to ride over to these sections, which were several miles off the road, and having an engagement in Adelaide on a certain day I was obliged to push on; I therefore procured the following description of

McConville's Mine,

WHICH comprises sections 1424 and 1455, about six miles South from Kanyaka, amongst low bald hills. There is a lode on the surface in both sections, running about 300 yards North and South, and about 18 inches thick; the Ore, which is mixed with gossan and felspar, is not continuous, but occurs in patches, it is a rich sulphuret, peculiar in appearance, and of a dark greenish grey color. A shaft was sunk on the lode to the depth of about three and a-half fathoms, and a drive was then carried for five fathoms, Copper Ore being obtained throughout. Some holes were sunk in other places and Copper found in all. Nine tons of Ore have been raised, a sample of which assayed 27½ per cent. Another claim which I omitted seeing is called

Malone's Mine,

AND is about eight miles from Watts's Sugarloaf. A lode containing stains of Copper was found on the surface, and on sinking some good Ore was met with. The country is favorable, and the lode contains good gossan with the Ore. Some very good samples of the Ore have been sent to Adelaide, and the claim is considered a promising one. But little work, however, has been done here yet.

I have now described all the principal Mines in the Northern part of the colony, and am not aware that I have omitted one of any importance, and which could fairly be called a Mine. However, I believe there are several valuable mineral claims, on which, at present, no work has been done; and which, from various causes, I did not visit. I do not consider that the omission of a notice of these claims is a matter of much importance, as connected with the object of the present work, and which, as I stated in the Introductory Chapter, was to give a description of the Mines of the colony. I have no intention of casting a slur upon those claims which I have not described, for I have no doubt there are some which I did not see as rich, or richer, than many which I have noticed. Had I attempted to describe every mineral claim in the colony, the bulk of the book would have been increased five-fold, and the price must have been in proportion, while the importance of the information would not have been adequate, and the work would, necessarily, have appeared extremely tedious. While, in many instances, the descriptions I have given will serve as a guide to persons desirous of investing in the Mines, the book has not been written with that view, and those who think of investing should satisfy themselves by other means of the eligibility of anything that may be offered to their notice.

On my return to Adelaide, after a few day's rest, I visited the Mines in the East and South, and these I now beg to introduce to the notice of the reader. The first I shall describe is

The Bremer Mine.

THIS Mine is the freehold property of the Worthing Mining Company, and is sometimes called the Callington Mine—Callington being the name of the surrounding township, which has sprung up since the discovery of the Mine. It was first discovered in 1850, and is 36 miles from Adelaide, on the bank of the Bremer, a considerable creek, running into the Murray ; though only a chain of brackish waterholes in summer. The surrounding country is flat, consisting of clayslate, shaly rock, micaceous schist, and occasionally a little quartz. The present state of the workings may be thus described :—The engine-shaft is sunk to a depth of 53 fathoms, and levels have been driven at the following depths—12, 23, 33, and 43 fathoms, on the course of the lode, North 23 ° West. The total length of the drives is above 400 fathoms. Some fine courses of Ore have been met with five and six feet wide, but occasionally rather dradgey ; however, at the lower levels there has been a decided improvement in this respect, fine yellow Ore, of a quality superior to most of what has hitherto been raised, as well as more solid in the lode, being now in course of working at the 53-fathom cross-cut. The Ores in this Mine are sulphurets of a good average quality ; the prevailing Ore is yellow, there is also black, and a little peacock met with. 4,500 tons of Ore have been raised here in five years, the large proportion of which has been obtained during the last two years. The large engine is a very fine one of 60-inch cylinder ; a smaller engine (40 horse-power) works the machinery, and will be used for hauling. The smelting works, under the management of the Messrs. Thomas, are about 250 or 300 yards from the Mine, and comprise one calcining and two smelting furnaces. The Copper made is of the quality of 96 per cent. of pure Copper, the refining process being omitted.

Notwithstanding the small average produce of the Ores—only 13 per cent.—lower, I believe, than any other Mine in the colony, this Mine is made to pay owing to the very careful management adopted by Alfred Hallett, Esq , who devotes a considerable portion of his time to the personal supervision of the Mine. Everything is done with strict economy, and the important principle, " let nothing be wasted or lost," is fully carried out. Machinery is made largely available for reducing the Ores, and thus a Mine, which must at once show a loss if worked as other Mines in the colony are worked, is rendered profitable to the proprietors, besides providing direct employment for 120 hands, including smelters ; and indirectly providing the means of living for three or four times that number. That useful and recently invented machine, known as " Appleton's Stonebreaker," is employed for crushing the inferior Ores preparatory to their being sorted, the best of the Ore having been previously broken and picked by hand, when it is sent to the crushing rollers to prepare it for the furnace. The " smalls" are dealt with as usual, being jigged and washed. The most important machinery for washing the smalls and the slime Ores is in use at this Mine, consisting of a con-continuation of Vyan's Rake Buddle, self-acting plunge jiggers, and the revolving table, hitherto only used for washing lead Ores, has been adapted by Mr. Hallett for separating the slime, and is found to answer admirably. It is, perhaps, scarcely necessary to give a description of this machinery in a work like the present, but from what I saw of its performances I am convinced that its use in other Mines would add a considerable percentage to the profits, and would enable some Mines to be profitably worked, which at present yield nothing to the proprietors. Many of our Mine adventurers would derive a useful lesson, and more than one, perhaps, from a visit to the Bremer Mine. There has been no extravagant outlay in handsome buildings, and "no more cats are kept than catch mice," yet everything absolutely necessary appears to be provided. I look upon this as the model Mine of South Australia, and its enterprising Manager, Mr. Hallett, deserves the highest praise for the judicious and persevering manner in which he has developed the property, in spite of difficulties that would have disheartened many.

From the Bremer Mine I proceeded through pretty country, to another property belonging to the same Company, and called

The Preamimma Mine.

THIS Mine is about six miles North-East of Callington, and on a rather high hill, in generally hilly country, near the Murray Scrub, 38 miles from Adelaide. Some fine surface indications were found here, and the Mine was opened in 1854, some good Ore being raised, chiefly carbonates ; after a time the lode was lost, and the Mine abandoned. The present proprietary commenced reworking this Mine about two years since. They carted away 100 tons of stuff, from the surface, to their smelting works, to use as flux, and this yielded five tons of Copper. Several tons of "roughs" are still scattered about, and, if gathered up, would probably produce 10 per cent. of Copper. The engine-shaft is sunk to a depth of above 47 fathoms, and some fine black Ore was cut, about 30 fathoms from the surface, but not in paying quantities. It was, however, believed, from certain indications, that a good lode would be met with at about 45 or 50 fathoms, and the appearance of the ground at the present depth strengthens that opinion. Some rich grey and black Ore is now being raised from the engine-shaft ; and quantities of Mundic have been met with almost throughout the entire course of the sinking. Some muriate of Copper has also been found in this Mine.

This is one of the old mining districts of the colony, and from the quantities of Ore that are now being raised here, and the still larger quantities that are evidently likely to be produced, I think my readers will agree with me, that it is to be regretted that operations once commenced, in so favorable a country, were ever abandoned. Several promising Mines opened in this district during the years 1845–6, and 7, and from which large quantities of rich Ores were raised were closed, chiefly, I believe, for want of judicious management. Some of these have been taken up again during the last two or three years, and appear to be working advantageously, and with excellent prospects. The first of these Mines, which I propose to notice, is the original South Australian Company's Mine,

The Kanmantoo Mine.

It is is about three miles nearer Adelaide than the Bremer Mine, being a little to the South of East from the City, and amongst hilly country. The present Company was formed in November, 1861, with a capital of £12,000, in £5 shares ; £2 of which only has yet been called up. Since the commencement of this Company, 1,920 tons of Ore have been raised, and smelted at the Company's smelting works, in the neighborhood of Scott's Creek. These works consist of a calcining, a reverberatory, and a refining furnace, and other necessary buildings. The principal lodes are the Kangaroo, Emily's, and the Boundary lode. The two former run North and South, and the latter is a counter lode. The first is a large lode yielding yellow Ore of a moderate percentage. Emily's lode has produced large quantities of yellow Ore, which, at the 10-fathom level, gave place to red oxide and native Copper ; one large block sent to Adelaide for exhibition weighed 11 cwt. Two levels have been driven on the lode, at 16 and 26 fathoms, respectively, showing a considerable quantity of Ore to have been left in the Mine. The Copper produced at the smelting works from the Ore now being raised amounts to about 12 tons per month, and the rate of cartage to Adelaide is 20s. per ton. A large amount of work has been done at this Mine since its first commencement. The South Australian Company raised about 4,000 tons of Ore, and opened a large extent of ground. Mr. W. B. Dawes, who subsequently rented the Mine, raised above 1,900 tons. Some of the old stopes and drives in the Mine testify, on examination, to the immense deposits of Ore which formerly existed there. This Mine is paying the proprietors. Sixty-four hands are at present employed on it, and 16 at the smelting works. There is a small but flourishing township about half a mile from the Mine, and called after the native name of the place—whence also the Mine derived its designation—Kanmantoo.

A short distance from this, on an adjoining section, is another Mine, called

The West Kanmantoo Mine.

THE workings are on the side of a hill about 100 feet above the valley. A very large opening—part of former workings—exists in the ground, and from this a large quantity of Ore was taken. At the time of my visit only two men were at work at the bottom of this opening at a depth of 10 fathoms, and they had just cut a seam of fine black Ore, which looked both rich and promising for quantity. Since then the quantity raised by the two men in two months was 30 tons. Some good carbonates have been found in another part of the Mine, and the prospects are considered highly satisfactory. A royalty is paid by the present company on the Ore raised.

In the neighborhood of the Bremer and Kanmantoo Mines are several others, that have been worked to a certain extent, but as they are at present shut up and contain no features, as far as I am aware, requiring special notice, I do not deem it necessary to allude to them all, even by name. Of these the most important was the Paringa Mine, from which nearly 900 tons of Copper Ore were raised, and which, probably, may at some future time again be worked to advantage. Indeed, this is so evidently a mineral district, and one, the position of which, offers so many advantages that, under circumstances of capital and labor different from those at present obtaining in the colony, I should not be surprised to see many of these old Mines tried again. There are also other Mines between the Bremer and Adelaide—at Lobethal, Hahndorf, &c.—in fact it is impossible to travel far in the hills without coming into the neighbourhood of metallic Ores of some kind, even if only iron.

About ten miles from this Mine, and 32 from Adelaide, is

The Wheal Ellen Mine,

SITUATED amongst hilly country about three miles from Strathalbyn. The property, which comprises 700 acres, is freehold. It was originally worked solely as a Silver-lead Mine, and some fine lodes of galena and carbonates were opened, yielding from eight to ten tons of the former and five of the latter per fathom. About 2,000 tons of Lead Ore were raised containing, besides 90,000 ounces of Silver, and from one to two ounces of Gold in each ton of pig-lead. A very large quantity of auriferous gossan is found in this Mine, which has yielded, on assay in England, from four to six ounces of Gold to the ton. Four thousand tons of Ore are estimated to be in reserve in the present levels.

The lode is opened on for a length of 120 fathoms. Six shafts have been sunk to various depths, and levels driven every ten fathoms. Bassett's shaft is 62 fathoms in depth, and at the 50 the lode is larger than at any other part of the Mine. Scott's shaft is sunk 45 fathoms, the bottom going down in galena and blended with yellow Ore. The engine-shaft is down 30 fathoms and fully prepared for the engine and pit work now on the ground and ready to be erected. Spence's shaft has also been sunk 30 fathoms through a large lode of iron gossan, bearing Gold for about 22 fathoms, when rich red oxide of Copper made its appearance, and in the lowest depth the gossan has given place to mundic, containing about 4 per cent. of Copper. The North pit shaft is sunk 22 fathoms, and communicates with Spence's for the sake of ventilation. From the nature of the ground, and the fine lode of Ore already discovered, large returns of Copper are expected from this part of the Mine ; it is now being worked on tribute at a good profit. At the present time the water is in the Mine up to just above the 40 fathom level, below which there are large reserves of Ore which cannot be raised until the engine is erected.

Operations at this Mine are just now very slack, pending certain negociations, in England, respecting the property.

A fine large chimney-stack, connected with the smelting furnaces, rises to a height of about 70 feet ; and the furnaces consist of a calcining and reverberatory furnace, also a complete blast furnace, with a steam-engine, and every requisite. The supply of timber for smelting purposes is likely to be inexhaustible for very many years to come ; it is now being delivered at 4s. 6d. per ton on the Mine !

Not far from the Wheal Ellen is the batch of Mines known as the Monster Lode Mineral property, and the old Stralhalbyn Mines.

The Monster Lode Property

CONSISTS of several mineral sections, upon which a number of places have been opened, yielding Copper Ore. A small party of miners have been working on tribute, on some of these sections, during the past six months, and have raised sufficient Ore to justify the expectation that if capital were employed in developing the property it might be added to the list of our *bonâ fide* Mines.

The Strathalbyn Mines

COMPRISE a property consisting of 635 acres of low hilly land, which, unlike most of that on which the Mines are situated, is fit for agricultural purposes. These mines were originally opened by private enterprise about the year 1848, and some quantity of good Copper Ore was raised and smelted on the property. It was subsequently sold to an English Company, who made preparations apparently with the intention of carrying on operations on an extensive scale, but this they never did, and the Copper lodes, for the working of which they originally purchased the property, have remained almost, if not entirely, untouched, the water not even having been pumped out. On another section a lode of Silver-lead has been opened and several hundred tons of the Ore were sent to England. In one place, about 18 fathoms below the surface, a splendid lode, 18 feet wide, of solid galena is exposed, and this lode having been traced for about 30 fathoms it is estimated that fully 2,000 tons of Ore can be taken out. The Ore contains about $18\frac{1}{2}$ per cent. of lead, and $16\frac{1}{2}$ ounces of Silver to the ton. The shaft here is sunk about 30 fathoms, and in the bottom the galena is improving, and is also impregnated with yellow Copper Ore. There is a portable steam engine on the Mine, and the pump work is there ready for immediate use —it is really a pity to see such a property lying idle.

Coming nearer to Adelaide we find the old

Montacute Mine,

On the Mount Lofty Range, and about 10 miles nearly North-east from Adelaide. This Mine was discovered in 1843-4, and the section on which it was found was purchased at auction by Messrs. Baker, Frederick Dutton, Hagen, and Hart, for the sum of £1,550 ; a few hours afterwards they parted with three-tenths of their interest for what the whole had cost them, and the company formed was called the Montacute Mining Company. The Mine is situated on a steep spur of the range, and extensive out-croppings of Ore were visible on the surface. The Ores are chiefly yellow and peacock Ores, averaging about 18 per cent. ; some native Copper was also found. The Mine was worked for some time and several hundreds of tons of Ore raised, but it has now been for many years abandoned. Other sections in the neighborhood also contain Copper. About three miles North-east of the Montacute, another Copper Mine was discovered and purchased by G. A. Anstey, Esq., of Highercombe, but little work was done, and the Mine having been long since abandoned, it scarcely demands a lengthened notice. Some Mines of more importance, and which for some years, while worked, yielded a good return of Silver-lead Ore, are

The Glen Osmond Mines,

A little more than four miles from Adelaide. They are the property of Osmond Gilles, Esq., who leased them on a royalty to an English company. There are several good lodes in the ground, and many hundred tons of Ore were raised, yielding about 70 per cent. of lead and from 15 to 18 ounces of silver to the ton; but I believe the royalty was found to be too high to leave the lessees sufficient profit, and other causes combined to cause the abandonment of the works. The country consists of a very hard clayslate.

The Wheal Watkins Lead Mines, adjoining the above, were for a short time worked successfully; and the Mines of the Wheal Gawler Mining Company were also, at one time, amongst our working Mines. The late Mr. Duncan McFarlane also had a lead Mine a short distance up Glen Osmond.

In other directions, I have heard of recent discoveries of Copper: on the Para, about 12 or 14 miles from Adelaide, on the Uley Hills, to the East of Gawler, and elsewhere in the neighborhood of Gawler; also on Skilligolee Creek, a few miles from Auburn; but it will be impossible for me to visit and write about these places in the present work. I am informed that one man in the Uley Hills makes a very fair living by carting to the Smelting Works, at Port Adelaide, the Copper Ore which he scrapes up on the surface of his own land; and I believe the same has been done by others, without any *mining* at all.

The next locality I shall describe is the

Scott's Creek Mine,

ABOUT 18 miles from Adelaide, near Cherry Gardens. It is on the side of a steep but not very high hill, on the surface of which in ironstone rock some strong stains of Copper were found. A shaft was sunk, and some good stones of rich Ore were raised, chiefly grey oxide, mixed with a little green and blue carbonate. The lode was small but regular and well defined; at the depth of five fathoms there was but little Ore, the lode being composed chiefly of gossan. The same lode has been found on the opposite side of the section, but a sufficient depth has not yet been reached to enable a judgment to be formed as to the future of this Mine. The ground looks favorable, and the lode is nearly a downright one, having but little underlay; a creek of good water runs through the section and timber is plentiful.

It is not my intention in describing the Southern Mines to enter into such particulars respecting the appearance of the country, or the mode of travelling, as I did when writing on the Northern Mines, for these more settled districts are better known to residents in the colony; and for the information of readers in England and elsewhere, I may state generally that the South comprises a large extent of agricultural land, in most

instances presenting pleasing features to the eye, farms, home-
steads, and rural townships being thickly scattered through the
country ; the scene is diversified occasionally by scrub or a belt
of stringy bark forest, which, in its turn, gives place to scenery
of great natural beauty, this being often increased by the presence of a pretty farmhouse with its beautiful garden, &c , or by
a neat township, with its church, mill, and scattered dwellings.

Twenty-one miles from Adelaide, we arrive at the township of
Noarlunga, through which flows the Onkaparinga, the second
river, as to importance, in the colony. Mineral has been found
in several places in this neighborhood, but no Mine of any note
has been worked here since the Worthing Mine, about five miles
nearer Adelaide, in Morphett Vale. That Mine was at one time
believed to promise well; but the country was extremely hard,
and Ore not being found in paying quantities, it was abandoned.
After passing sundry smaller townships, and numerous farms,
and some scrub and forest land, we reach Yankalilla, 50 miles
from Adelaide, and one of the prettiest, and most substantial, of
all our country towns. It is beautifully situated in a fine valley,
about two miles from the sea. Leaving Yankalilla, and travelling
seawards, we come to Normanville, a smaller township, boasting,
however, the possession of the district Court House. About a
mile and a half nearly North from Normanville; a Silver-lead
Mine called

Barritt's Mine,

Is being worked by private enterprise; Mr. Butterworth, I
believe, being associated with Mr. Barritt in the venture. This
Mine is on a hill, in sight of the sea. It was first discovered
in July, 1862, and in about five months three men had sunk a
shaft 10 fathoms, and driven 11 on a rather irregular course of
Ore. They had raised 15 tons of Ore, 10 of which were shipped.
I was informed that it was rich in silver, and yielded 2¼ ozs. of
Gold to the ton. They had been driving North-East and South-
West ; but the indications of a North and South lode appeared
to me to be stronger, and the men informed me that a similar
opinion had been expressed by some one else, and that they were
going to try in that direction. The country consists of clayslate
and limestone.

Two miles South of Normanville there is a Copper-bearing
lode on Mr. David Cowan's property, and he calls it

The Gorge Mine.

It is on the face of a steep hill, rising almost abruptly from a
flat half a mile from the sea. The lode runs about N.N.E., and
is traceable for above 250 yards on the surface. It is composed

of a quartzose rock strongly stained and impregnated with blue and green carbonate of Copper, and containing thin veins of Ore. As the lode runs in the direction of the range, it would be easy to cut it by means of an adit driven in at the foot of the hill. The outcropping of the Ore is about 100 feet above the level of the sea, and the indications and nature of the country appear favorable ; and should a valuable Mine be developed here it will derive many advantages from its proximity to a place of shipment, from its situation in the midst of a large agricultural district, and from the abundance of fuel and water in the neighbourhood ;—there are two creeks of fresh water on the land.

There are other mineral discoveries in the vicinity, but none of them have yet been developed.

The Yattagolinga Mine.

A few miles farther South, at Rapid Bay, a Lead and Copper Mine was discovered and purchased by Mr. H. W. Phillips, in February, 1844. The lodes of lead are close to the surface, and are easily worked. The produce was 75 per cent. of Lead and from 22 to 25 oz. of Silver per ton. The Copper lodes were found cropping out on the surface, and showing also in the face of the cliffs fronting the sea, at a depth of 400 or 500 feet from the top. The Ores consisted of grey, yellow, and peacock Ores. About 50 tons of Silver-lead Ore were raised. The workings were stopped partly from want of proper superintendence, and partly because the Messrs. Phillips gave up a station which they had held in the neighbourhood. I am informed that they have recently been applied to by practical miners for permission to work the ground on tribute. The ground is rather hard, but the situation cannot be surpassed for the facilities which it affords for dressing and shipping away the Ore—a stream of water constantly running through the valley at the foot of the Mine. Some fine white marble is found on this and the adjoining land. There are also other mineral deposits in the neighborhood, but no great amount of work has been done here. The country is very pretty ; but between this place and Cape Jervis, a distance of nearly 10 miles, a belt of stringy-bark forest intervenes, relieved towards the coast by beautiful and fertile valleys. On the high ranges, about two miles East from the Cape, we come to the

Campbell's Creek Silber-lead Mines,

Comprising seven sections of land. Lead has been found in various places on the property, but no payable lode has yet been cut. Drives have been made in four different places, and something like a lode was found, but not very well defined; and although the Ore was good it was not in sufficient quantities; yet the Talisker Mine was working a payable lode, apparently running in the direction of this section, and at a distance of only 40 fathoms. On section 1610 a drive was carried eight fathoms and stopped for want of hands, some good stones of Ore, however, were raised, and a pile of several hundredweight was at grass. Another drive was made on 1558, and carried eight and a half fathoms, with the view of cutting the Talisker lode North, and which, it was hoped, would be accomplished when about 22 fathoms more had been driven.

Although, hitherto, the operations on these claims have not been very successful, it is not improbable that the lodes turning out so well in the Talisker Mine may make in depth in the ground worked by the Campbell's Creek Company.

As I have already intimated, closely adjoining these claims are those of the

Talisker Silver-lead Mine.

THESE claims comprise about the same extent of ground as the Campbell's Creek Mine, but the proprietors have been much more fortunate in their operations. The principal workings are on section 1554. An adit level, the lower cross-cut, was driven four fathoms into the hill; the upper cross-cut being at the same time driven 18 fathoms, and intersecting a fine lode, running North-east and South-west, containing above 75 per cent. of Lead, and from 35 to 40 ozs. of Silver to the ton of Ore. This cross-cut intersected the lode, and was then driven on its course for four fathoms each way. A winze was sunk on the course of the lode, in the lower or South level, and an air-shaft sunk from above nearly six fathoms. This part of the ground presented a very favorable appearance, the lode was looking settled, and shewed good quantities of fine Ore. Since my visit I understand, from disinterested parties who have seen the Mine, that a material improvement has taken place here; and I can readily believe it, as it is no more than might have been expected from the general appearance of the ground. What is called Mufford's level has been driven about 12 fathoms on the course of the lode, and a winze been sunk four fathoms to open up ground for stoping; the lode here being nearly five feet wide of almost solid Ore. When I visited the Mine nearly 100 tons of Ore were at grass. The first shipment of about 20 tons had just been made, and the remainder was being sorted and dressed. Since then two further shipments have been made, and a large quantity of Ore raised. Machinery is now (March) in course of erection for dressing the Ore, and the prospects of the Mine are very encouraging. The works are under the superintendence of Messrs. Alfred Jenkin & Son.

Three or four miles from the Talisker, Silver-lead Ore has been discovered on the property of Mr. P. B. Coglin, M.P., but no work has yet been done to develop the extent of the discovery. Both Lead and Copper are also said to exist in other places in the neighborhood, and it is not improbable that ere long this part of the country may become an important mineral district. The facilities for shipment are very great, and Mines could be made to pay here that would be worthless far in the interior.

Leaving this part of the country, I now proceed to notice briefly another mineral district which should, perhaps, according to geographical arrangement, have been alluded to before—I refer to Angaston, Truro, and the North Rhine.

Prior to the year 1846, a German Geologist, Mr. Menge, well known at that time in this colony, discovered a lode on a section belonging to George Fife Angas, Esq., near Angaston, and in the valley of the river Gawler. There were indeed two lodes, one of which was traced for above 200 yards, and some fine samples were raised yielding, on assay, 33 per cent. of Copper; but no systematic mining was prosecuted here. Subsequently another very promising Mine, the Wheal Barton, was found on another part of Mr. Angas's estate, or in the immediate neighbourhood, and for a time it created quite a stir in the colony, but from some cause or other, either mismanagement or want of unanimity amongst the shareholders—for a company was formed for working it—it was closed; although it is believed by many that it would have proved a very valuable and remunerative Mine. I am informed there is a probability of its being again worked before very long.

More recently, a new discovery was made close to the township of Angaston, and called the Crinnis Mine. The late Captain Rodda entertained a very favorable opinion of the place; but after an ephemeral existence the Company formed for working the property was broken up.

About 10 miles from Angaston, on fine, thinly timbered, and moderately hilly country, we find

The North Rhine Mine.

THIS Mine is situated on sections 563 and 570, the Company having, also, the adjoining sections numbered 550 and 562—all freehold. Copper is found on the whole of the land, and one of the lodes is traced through two sections. There are two lodes running nearly parallel, in a North and South direction, with an underlay towards the West of about 18 inches in the fathom. The Ores found near the surface were green and blue carbonates of promising appearance. The Eastern lode was first opened; and about 20 tons of Ore, averaging a little over 20 per cent. of Copper, were sent to England, but as the water soon became too strong to be kept in fork by animal power, an engine-shaft was sunk near the main (or Nicholls') lode, and a 70 horse power engine and pump work fixed; this has been working very efficiently since March, 1860. Another shaft, near the engine-shaft, had been commenced prior to the present Company taking the Mine, and this was continued by Captain Barker, until the lode was cut at 20 fathoms, where it was four feet wide, being composed of black Ore, Mundic, and spar. The sinking was continued to 30 fathoms, and it was after this that the engine-shaft was sunk. The lode was, unfortunately, not found to yield Ore in paying quantities when cut again at the 30-fathom level; but the indications were deemed such as to warrant further sinking. When the 43-fathom level was reached a drive was made and carried on for 70 fathoms on the course of the lode; but although the lode varied from three to six feet in width, it contained too large a proportion of Mundic to allow of its being worked to advantage. The engine-shaft has been sunk to a depth of 60-fathoms, and another drive made for 50 fathoms, but the lode unfortunately remains unremunerative, although containing black sulphuret throughout. The drive is being continued, in order to communicate with a winze which is in course of sinking from the 43-fathom level.

Before proceeding to a description of the extraordinary Mines on Yorke's Peninsula, and most generally known as the Wallaroo and Moonta Mines, I may make a passing allusion to the fact of Copper Mines having been for some time worked on the opposite peninsula, to the Westward, and in the neighborhood of Port Lincoln. One of these Mines was called the Mount Liverpool, and another the Port Lincoln Mine; a fair amount of good Ore has at different times been raised from these Mines, but, I am informed, the hardness of the ground is one obstacle in the way of their being profitably worked. Some persons still assert that, under good management, and with labor at a reasonable rate, they might yet be worked to advantage.

I believe Plumbago has been found in considerable quantities in this neighborhood; it is also traceable for three miles along a range near Gumeracha.

In a work on the Mines of the Colony, I should hardly be justified in omitting to notice our little Gold-field at Echunga, 20 miles from Adelaide, although a Victorian or New South Wales digger would perhaps not exchange one good claim in the richer colonies for the whole of our diggings. These diggings were discovered about 10 or 11 years ago, and ever since that time a few plodding persevering men have continued to

work here, and although no great "finds" have been made, very
good average wages have been earned, and, in the aggregate, some
thousands of pounds worth of gold raised annually. It is next to
impossible to arrive at an accurate estimate of the total quantity,
for those who have evidently been most successful have been
very quiet—keeping their own counsel.

Gold has been found in many other parts of the Colony, and a
recent discovery has been announced at the Meadows, a few miles
from Echunga, but the extent of the auriferous ground is not yet
ascertained. I have seen a sample of the Gold, which is more
shotty than that found at Echunga, the latter being remarkably
fine and flaky. Gold has also been met with in quartz reefs
here, but none of the attempts to work them have hitherto been
successful.

It is singular that, up to the present time, this Colony should
have proved the poorest in the precious metal, as I believe the
first Gold discovered in Australasia was found in one of our
oldest Copper Mines, in the Mount Lofty ranges, about 17 years
ago. If I remember rightly, a brooch was made from the Gold,
and sent as a present to Her Majesty the Queen, the Mine being
called the Victoria Mine.

The Wallaroo Mines.

LITTLE more than three years since, some excitement was caused
in Adelaide by the announcement that a valuable discovery of
Copper had been made on Captain W. W. Hughes's sheep run
at Wallaroo. Copper had been found on the Peninsula years
before; but the small attempts made at the time to trace the
lode were not so successful as to lead to any extended operations.
The excitement I have alluded to did not at once become
general, but before many months had elapsed there was a perfect
furore for securing "claims" at Wallaroo. To such an extent
did this proceed, that, to my knowledge, persons who had never
seen the place went to the Land Office and asking to see the
plans, indicated two or three spots where they desired to take
out claims; and some of these "dips in the lucky bag" resulted
satisfactorily! I think I should scarcely exaggerate if I were to
say that hundreds of claims were taken out for no other reason
than they were North, South, East, or West, of some other
claim said to contain Copper! Some really good discoveries
were made, and many persons who undertook a systematic search
for mineral on the Peninsula were well rewarded for their
trouble. But, notwithstanding all the "splendid prospects," I
think I shall not be wrong in saying that not more than half a
dozen out of the hundreds of "promising Mines" on Yorke's
Peninsula shew at the present time any prospect of proving

remunerative; and not even half that number are as yet actually paying. Still this is a wonderful mineral district, and when the bad effects of the mania shall have passed away, and mining is pursued in a legitimate and less speculative way, it may be that still greater riches may be brought to light. Of course the Treasury benefitted largely by the unexpected influx of wealth, derived from the rents of so many sections; besides two large townships were laid out and the land sold at a high price; but, as usual, the proceeds of the whole were absorbed in the general revenue, and the locality which had added so much to the public funds received the usual amount of official neglect in return. The inhabitants complain, and very justly, that nothing has been done by the Government to improve their roads; and notwithstanding the scheme for drainage—so essential to the successful prosecution of mining at Wallaroo—which was laid before Parliament, no action has been taken, and the working of one really valuable Mine has been stopped in consequence of the "mad-water." Acres are covered, for a depth of two or three feet, with water pumped out of the Mines, and which must soon porcolate back through the light porous soil. Besides this evil, the health of the inhabitants is likely to suffer from the amount of stagnant water which can find no natural outlet. The Surveyor-General, in his report, estimated that at least a fair interest on the cost of constructing a drain would be readily paid by the Mining Companies—yet nothing is done. Perhaps the present Parliament will move in the matter.

Private enterprise is generally in advance of Governments, and so it has proved at Wallaroo, for a railway has been constructed from the Mines to the Port, a distance of about five miles, by Mr. A. H. Gouge, the Peto of South Australia. Since Mr. Gouge got the railway into working order, a Company has purchased it, Mr. Gouge, however, retaining a considerable share. It is in contemplation to extend a branch from Port Wallaroo to the Moonta Mines (9 miles) as the present line is paying handsomely. I should also state that a fine jetty has been constructed at the Port, so that although close in shore the water is shoal, vessels of 1,000 tons can load and discharge in safety at the jetty, which is connected with the railway.

Before commencing a description of the Mines, I may state that the two townships contain many very substantial buildings, the hotels being equal to any in Adelaide. The population of the Peninsula, which three years ago consisted of a few shepherds, besides Captain Hughes and his family, in a few months after the opening of the Mines began to be reckoned by thousands; the number of the inhabitants at the present time is somewhere about 6,000.

The land is low and undulating, and, in the latitude of the Mines, it stretches for about 30 miles between the two gulfs. The soil is loose and sandy, and abundance of limestone is found in nodules and blocks on the surface. This part of the Peninsula is well-grassed, in large patches of pasture land, surrounded by mallee scrub. K

The first Mine which attracts the attention of the traveller proceeding from Clinton, or Port Arthur, to Wallaroo, is "The Cumberland," which is prettily situated to the left (South) of the road, on open rising ground, surrounded by scrub. The buildings of the Mine are plainly seen from the road, although about a mile and a half distant. Soon after the working of this Mine was commenced, what appeared to be a fine lode was discovered on the surface, but it proved to be only a boil, and ran out in about three fathoms. Some fine Galena was also met with in a similar way. A considerable amount of work was done with the view of finding the lost lode, but without success. Three shafts were sunk, one of which was, at the time, the deepest on the Peninsula, viz., 27 fathoms; and many fathoms of drives were made, besides costeening. Above eight tons of good Ore, altogether, was raised here; but eventually the Mine was abandoned. I shall not pretend to enumerate, much less to give a notice of, all the "Mines" started in this district. I may, however, briefly allude to some of the unsuccessful ones, and amongst these are "The Finniss Claims," which really deserved to have resulted in a good Mine, from the patient, untiring perseverance displayed by the unfortunate proprietors. If some others had pursued as legitimate and systematic a course of genuine mining, in search of Ore, as did the Finniss Claims' Company, the state of affairs in connection with their pockets and their claims might have been very different from what it is.

One of the first Mines which commenced working at Wallaroo after the original Wallaroo Mines was

The New Cornwall,

WHICH was introduced to the public with very good prospects. The Mine is about a mile E S.E. from Kadina. It is now about two years since this Mine was opened by the present Company, and during the former part of the time operations were pursued with great vigor; several shafts were sunk, drives cut, and stoping done. There are two main lodes—Lucas's and Sismey's; the former is the principal. They are almost parallel lodes, running nearly North-West and South-East, but converging both as to their direction and their underlay. All the veins and strings of Ore met with also converge towards the main lode; it is therefore expected, that where the lodes meet there will be a very large deposit of Ore. Lucas's lode has varied in width from one to 14 feet. Squarey's (Engine) shaft is now sunk to a depth of 29 fathoms on Sismey's lode, and No. 2 shaft, on the same side, is down 20 fathoms; a cross-cut is being driven from this level to intersect Lucas's lode. This is considered one of the leading points of the Mine, as, eight fathoms below the surface, the lode was opened on for a length of 15 fathoms, presenting a strong and promising appearance, and containing quartz, green carbonate, and muriate of Copper. The cross-cut now being made will cut the lode at 12-fathoms lower. The lodes at present are not first-rate courses of Ore, but disturbed and dradgey. There was a considerable influx of water in this cross-cut, but arrangements are being made to put the machinery in order to keep it in fork. Unfortunately, an accident, similar to what occurred some time since, has recently happened to the engine; and to prevent a recurrence of it the engine will have to be reset, which will cause the works to be suspended for about a month. The country in Squarey's engine-shaft is as favorable in appearance as could be desired, and contains some good stones of Ore and pieces of native Copper. The ground throughout the Mine is generally favorable.

I must not omit to mention that a large block of Ore, said to weigh nearly five tons, was sent to the International Exhibition of 1862, having been raised from Lucas's lode, out of White's Shaft. Between 3,000 and 4,000 tons of stuff are now at grass, and will be dressed up so as to yield, probably, from 800 to 1,000 tons of Ore, worth 15 per cent. of Copper. The buildings on the Mine are substantial—being, chiefly, of stone and brick—and comprise Captain's house, store, office, smith's and carpenter's workshops, besides engine-house and chimney-stack (72 feet high), also crushing-house, with a separate engine to work up to 12-horse power, driving two feet rollers. There is, also, a still for distilling water, and a tank to hold 15,000 gallons, stone stables, and several miners' cottages. Close at hand is Mr. Rodda's smelting establishment, which will be described in another place.

Though the prospects, or rather, I should say, the present position of the Mine is anything but satisfactory Captain East, who is evidently a very intelligent, practical man, entertains the best hopes for the future, and I think not without good reason. I trust, for the sake of the shareholders, these anticipations may be realized. I should recommend them not to sell out; but to hold their shares for another six months at least.

The Matta Matta Mine.

THIS is one of the richest of the batch of Mines near Kadina, and known as the Wallaroo Mines. Two shafts have been sunk to the depth of 20 fathoms. A fine lode of Ore was cut at the 10-fathom level, running about E.S.E. and W.N.W., consisting of rich green carbonate and grey sulphuret, with red oxide and a quantity of malleable Copper. Ore to the value of nearly £20,000 was raised; but, as the sinking proceeded, a large influx of water interfered with the work, the little engine of 25-horse power being unable to keep it in fork; but, perhaps, it would be more correct to say that, for want of sufficient drainage, the water found its way back into the Mine, and at present operations are suspended. It is singular that this Mine is so much wetter than the neighboring Mines, but so it is. There is scarcely any difference in the level of the ground, but the sub-strata must be looser, or some extraordinary spring of water must exist in the Mine. It is much to be regretted that operations were stopped here, for, as I said before, a fine productive lode was being worked, the Ore from which is far richer than that from any other Mines on the Peninsula, except the Moonta. The Matta Matta is prettily situated, in sight of Kadina, and Mr. E. K. Horn, the proprietor of half the property, has erected a neat and commodious cottage, which is occupied by his son, Mr. E. Horn, who has the management of the Mine. The necessary buildings in connection with the Mine are substantial. At one time about 40 hands were employed here.

A short distance to the North of West from the Matta are the original

Wallaroo Mines,

BETTER known by the names of the shafts, the "Home" and "Wombat." There are also Taylor's Engine Shaft, Young's Shaft, and Hughes's Engine Shaft; the last is the deepest, being down 40 fathoms. The Home Shaft is the next in point of depth, being down 24 fathoms; and the rest are all about 20 fathoms deep. There is also Smith's Shaft, which will not be used at present for want of sufficient drainage to carry off the water. The inconvenience suffered from want of drainage is manifest at all the Mines on the Peninsula, and unless some prompt action is taken in the matter it will become very serious. At these Mines Captain Warmington informs me that he has just been obliged to discharge twelve boys in order to allow of a pair of tributers washing their Ore; and this need not have been the case had the drainage been such as to admit of arrangements being made to enable the boys and tributers to work at the same time. Thus the poor lads are thrown out of employment, and the Mine is deprived of the benefit of their services.

The shafts I have named above are all sunk, at considerable intervals apart, on the same lode, running East and West, and a very considerable length of drives has been made on the course of the lode, besides a large amount of stoping having been done. In Hughes' shaft, at the 40-fathom level, a drive has been carried East on a splendid course of solid Ore, 8 feet in width. At the 30-fathom level and 20-fathom level, East of Hughes' shaft, there was an extraordinary course of Ore, the lode having opened out to a width of 30 feet of good yellow Ore, a little intermixed with spar, and having a very small "horse" in it, but worth nearly 60 tons to the fathom of Ore which would produce, as raised, probably 12 per cent. of Copper. This course of Ore had increased regularly from 10 feet wide at the 10-fathom level, to 20 feet at the 20, and so on. Ten fathoms turther East the lode is 8 feet wide of solid Ore. The prevailing nature of the Ore in this Mine is yellow sulphuret, but a variety of Ore has been met with in the course of the workings—red and grey oxides, carbonates and muriates, and a little malleable Copper. The average produce of the Ores from this Mine I suppose does not exceed 15 per cent, but the quantity is enormous, and the close proximity to a shipping port (5 miles) and the convenience of a railway passing within a few fathoms of the shafts, would enable the Mine to pay with a much lower produce. The extensive Smelting Works, erected at Port Wallaroo by the proprietors of this Mine, should also assist in increasing the profits of the undertaking. These will be noticed by-and-bye. There are two engines at present at work, both high-pressure, one of 24 and the other of 18 inch cylinder; the latter is used for crushing as well as pumping. An engine-house is just completed for the reception of a fine new Cornish pumping engine, recently imported, of 60 inch cylinder. This will work at Taylor's shaft.

Not to tire the reader with a more detailed description of the works at these wonderful Mines, the best account I can give of them is the following statement of the quantity of Ore raised : —

The total quantity of Ore sent away from the Mines, from the commencement to 31st January, this year, was 15,910 tons 12 cwt., and, probably, from 1,500 to 2,000 tons more are now at grass. About 300 men are employed, at wages varying from 4s. 6d. to 7s. 6d. per day.

About half a mile southward from the Wallaroo Mines we see the now abandoned " New Devon Mine," which was, for a time, worked with very good prospects of success ; some fine Ore was raised from a very promising branch lode, but it did not hold out. A little to the West of this, is

The Kurilla Mine,

WHERE some very good Ore was found near the surface, and a few tons raised; a lode was cut, underlying North about 15 inches in the fathom ; and a shaft sunk 25 fathoms. But little driving has been done ; at the 10-fathom level a drive of 15 feet cut the lode, containing branches of good Ore with micaceous slate and spar. Another drive was extended six fathoms West on the lode. The lode runs East and West, parallel with the Wallaroo lodes, and at the 25-fathom level it is nearly seven feet wide. A drive was carried 16 feet at the 15-fathom level, and cut the lode; it was then extended eight feet West, and four feet East on the lode, which contained branches of Ore. Eight tons of Ore, averaging over 25 per cent., were raised from the 10-fathom level, and altogether about 50 tons have been raised. At the 25-fathom level the lode contains some good branches of very fine yellow sulphuret Ore, and the prospects of the Mine are considered good. A small engine pumps the Mine, and there are good offices, and Captain's house, substantially built of stone.

About half a mile from the Kurilla, southwards, we come to

The Duryea Mine,

ON section 471. The Company to which this Mine belongs hold several other sections, as indeed do most of the Mining Companies; but no operations of importance are being carried on elsewhere, at present, though some of the other claims were considered to show good indications.

The Mine has now been worked above 18 months, and altogether several hundred tons of orey stuff have been raised, but the great bulk of it requires treating by some cheap and effectual process for separating the Ore, before it can be considered marketable. Twenty-five tons of 15 per cent. Ore were sold, and 25 more of probably a higher quality are ready for market, besides nearly five tons of 30 per cent., and about 50 or 60 which require dressing. The engine shaft is down above 37 fathoms, and is to be continued until 42 fathoms are reached. Cross-cuts and levels were driven at 12, 22, and 32 fathoms, and two regular lodes found, running nearly East and West, and underlying about 18 inches in the fathom. A very large amount of mundic has been met with in the lodes, and this is often an indication of a large amount of Copper below. The country is favorable, and some very good Ore has been found at various levels, and which may pay to stope away when the workings are in a more advanced state. A material improvement is perceptible in the cross-cut at the 32-fathom level where there is a good course of rich yellow and black Ore in the lodes, and where the two lodes appear to have run together. The appearance of the present end is very satisfactory; the country is evidently becoming more settled and with a little less mundic, and Ore in its place, the lode would soon prove payable. This it is confidently expected to do at the 42-fathom level.

The lode having steadily improved as it has gone down, and containing at the present level a promising course of fine yellow Ore in more settled country, it is only reasonable to conjecture that at the next level (42 fathoms) a still further improvement will be met with. There is a good deal of black Ore in veins and "squats" through the Mine, and some small branches of Ore, but in several places the Ore has been thrown out by "horses," or patches of unproductive ground. A great deal of Ore may be seen in small pieces intermixed with the stuff that has been hauled up from various parts of the lode, and if apparatus such as is employed at the Bremer Mine were brought to bear upon it, I think several tons of good marketable Ore might be recovered.

Proceeding from the Duryea Mine in the direction of Tipara, we see, about six miles on the road, a new claim called the Kangaroo, which is being worked by Mr. W. B. Dawes and others. When I saw it, on the 12th of March, no Ore had been cut, but the country looked remarkably "keenly," and there were indications which led to the supposition that they were not far from the back of the lode. Copper, in small quantities, has been found in the ground by the use of tests; but not in particles perceptible to the unaided eye, although small nodules have been smelted out of some of the stones, by Mr. Rodda's process. About a mile from the Kangaroo we come to the

Yelta Mine,

ON claims adjoining the Moonta, and where, for upwards of twelve months, operations have been vigorously carried on, in the hope of cutting the Moonta lodes. Small stones of Ore have occasionally been met with, and at one time it was thought that the same lode as was found in Buchan's shaft on the Moonta was cut in the Yelta. The country in some parts looks decidedly favorable for Copper, though it is hard in places. They are now driving at 11 fathoms, and an improvement in the ground is perceptible, and a good deal of steatite is making its appearance, and a "vug," or small cavity, containing fine Mundic, was found in the side of the drive. The proprietors feel very sanguine of ultimate success, and they deserve it for their patient perseverance. It would be surprising if the lodes stopped short on the Moonta claims, where they are strong and productive, and left the Yelta copperless. They surely must be found, perhaps at a greater depth, and the fact of a new and promising part of the lode, consisting of black and yellow Ore, having been cut in Buchan's shaft, is encouraging to the Yelta proprietors, as they also may meet with the same thing. The next Mines we come to are the celebrated

Moonta Mines,

THE great rivals of the world-renowed Burra Burra, which is described near the commencement of this work.

There are four distinct lodes on these Mines, all nearly parallel, within a space of half a mile, and running about North and South. The first discovery of Ore here was made about two years since, when a quantity of small stones of green carbonate was found on the surface. Some holes were sunk, and a lode of fine Ore cut at a small depth. This lode was named after one of the proprietors, Taylor's lode. Four shafts have since been sunk on it and named after proprietors ; Elder's, the deepest, is now 30 fathoms, and Smith's, Waterhouse's, and Taylor's, 20 fathoms each. A house for an engine of 60-inch cylinder is now in course of erection here for the purpose of pumping the Mine. In the drives from Smith's shaft a fine lode of yellow Ore, from 18 inches to 2 feet wide, is being worked at the 20-fathom level. The lode is $4\frac{1}{2}$ feet wide in Elder's shaft, in which shaft, at the 10-fathom level, a splendid lode of rich black Ore, largely mixed with malleable Copper, has yielded great quantities of Ore ; at one time it was being hauled up at the rate of 20 tons a day. From the drives from Taylor's shaft a quantity of rich Ore has been raised, consisting of black and grey sulphurets, red oxide, and malleable Copper.

The drives on the lode extend altogether for a length of about 350 fathoms at the 10 fathom levels, and for 250 fathoms at a depth of 20.

Two other lodes, Young's and MacDonnell's—the latter named after our late Governor—have produced Ore of a higher percentage than that from the other parts of these Mines ; it is grey sulphuret, some of which has given, on assay, 66 per cent. of fine Copper, and the average of the lodes is estimated at nearly 60 per cent. Both lodes have been driven on for a considerable distance at the 10-fathom levels, Young's being 6 feet wide, and MacDonnell's varying from 6 inches to 12 feet, but averaging a less width than Young's. At Buchan's shaft, a large deposit of malleable Copper and rich black Ore was met with, and some beautiful specimens of native dendritic and foliated Copper were found both here and on Taylor's lode. Buchan's shaft has been lately sunk to 20 fathoms, and a fine lode of black and yellow Ore cut.

The buildings on this Mine are large and substantial, and besides offices, stables, &c., comprise a complete and well-furnished assay office, under the management of Captain R. H. Hancock, a scientific gentleman who came to this colony a few years since to superintend the Wheal Ellen Mine.

The wonderful richness of these Mines will be seen from the following approximate return of Ore raised during twenty months, since the commencement of the workings, viz., 8,000 tons of Ore averaging nearly 25 per cent of pure Copper; and which has been raised at such a comparatively small cost as to enable two dividends of £10 per share each (together £64,000) to be declared on 1st October last, and 25th February this year.

The Miners say the Moonta will be a Mine when the Burra is forgotten—*because she* has lodes and the Burra has none ; but this remains to be proved. As long as one has plenty of gold it matters little whether it be in the shape of long bars or heaps of sovereigns.

About August or September last year, when a large quantity of Ore was required at Port Wallaroo for shipment, a distance of about 10 miles from the Moonta, 1,700 tons of Ore were delivered in nine days !—by means of drays. The number of hands employed on these Mines is nearly 300 ; but, until the last few months, not nearly so many were engaged. Ample provision is made for a supply of water, by means of large tanks holding many thousand gallons, collected from galvanized iron roofs. On an adjoining section, South of the Moonta, is the

Karkarilla Mine,

In the direct line of Taylor's lode, which has been cut here, and is now yielding fine yellow Ore, with some black; but at present scarcely in paying quantities. However, the lode is pretty regular, and improving as it goes down, so that when a few fathoms more are sunk it is probable there will be a good and profitable course of Ore. No. 1, Cudlip's shaft, is 26½ fathoms in depth, and the country looks very favorable; similar to that in the Moonta, and containing a great deal of steatite, which is regarded as a good indication. Drives have been carried, on the course of the lode, 24 fathoms South, and 12 fathoms North. Two or three small shafts were sunk at the commencement of operations here; but the main shaft, now, is No. 1, from which the workings are extended. In the present end of the drive the lode is about 15 inches wide, and is looking very well. About 15 tons of Ore, averaging 11½ per cent. of Copper, have been sold, and about 12 more, of a higher percentage, are now at grass. I can state, from my own examination of the Ore that was sold, that the low percentage must have arisen from its being imperfectly dressed, for what I saw bagged for market was very much mixed with spar and stone. This Mine is considered one of the substantial ones. Being in the hands of a few, and not very wealthy proprietors, it has been worked economically, and so much has not been done as might otherwise have been the case; but the proprietors are full of sanguine anticipations for the future.

About three and a half miles S.S.E. from the Karkarilla, a new claim has recently been opened under the name of the

Wheal Stuart,

About which there has been some little excitement in Adelaide, as it was represented to be a "second Moonta." I must confess I did not find the same amount of excitement in the immediate neighborhood. The claim is about three and a half miles S.S.E. of the Moonta, and a quantity of small pieces of green carbonate Ore was found on the surface. A shaft has been sunk for eight and a half fathoms, through gossan, steatite, ironstone, and quartz—all very favorable indications—and it is confidently hoped that the lode will soon be cut.

About four miles S.W. of the Moonta another discovery was made by Captain Lean, and although it has received no name intended to be permanent, it is pretty well-known as the

Wheal Humby,

BEING named after a storekeeper at Kadina, who has an interest in it. Similar surface indications to those at the Wheal Stuart and at the Moonta were found here, and on sinking four fathoms, the back of a lode was cut, consisting of ironstone, mixed with green carbonate of Copper. The country is good, being chiefly killas. It is difficult to say anything with reference to the probable future of either this or the preceding Mine. Present indications are undoubtedly good, and of course those interested are sanguine; but too little has at present been done to hazard the conjecture that they will be "second Moontas." I have noticed these claims as being the latest discoveries of any importance that I have heard of in the district; and, having now concluded my description of the Mines of South Australia, I proceed to notice

The Smelting Works.

THE Smelting Works immediately connected with some of the Mines, have been already briefly noticed, viz., those at the Kapunda, Bremer, Kanmantoo, Wheal Ellen, and Strathalbyn Mines. I do not conceive it necessary to observe any particular order, chronological or geographical, in describing the others. I may just mention two which are now matters of history only, having long since passed away—those near Port Adelaide, called the Yatala Smelting Works, and those at Apoinga, 22 miles from the Burra; but having just described the Wallaroo Mines, it may be as well, before taking leave of the Peninsula, to notice the Smelting Works here, and which are the most extensive in the colony, and the largest, I believe, out of Swansea. There are at present 22 furnaces, under a galvanized iron roof, measuring 695 feet in length, by 55 in breadth; 10 feet high to the wall-plate, and 18 feet to the ridge; besides a Refinery containing three furnaces, and measuring 80 feet by 50 feet in the clear, and 27 feet high. The sides of the shed over the furnaces being necessarily open, the roof is supported on massive stone arches. when rain falls an immense quantity of water is collected on so large a surface. Tanks are constructed to hold 50,000 gallons of water, and during a heavy shower the water from the roof completely fills the main pipe, of eight inches diameter, leading to the tanks. Eighteen furnaces are at present in operation, besides the three refining furnaces. Wood is burned in the latter, and in some of the others; the remainder burn coal. Over the furnaces is a tramway, leading from the place where the Ore is prepared for smelting, and the crushed Ore is put into a truck having a simple contrivance for tilting, so as to shoot the contents into the hoppers over the furnaces.

The building runs parallel with the beach, and close to the sea is a culvert six feet high, and six wide, built of stone and slabs of slag from the furnaces, moulded into the shape of bricks but much larger. This culvert, running parallel to the furnaces, receives the smoke from them, through flues passing downwards into it, and communicates with the chimney-stack by means of another culvert at right angles to it; a tremendous draft is thus obtained, and the heat generated is intense. We walked into a part of the culvert, and, through an aperture in a temporary party wall, could see, feel, and hear the effects of the tremendous blast of hot air rushing through.

The chimney-stack is a fine pile of bricks and mortar, being 120 feet in height, 24 feet square at the base, and 12 feet at the summit. The walls at the lower part are 5 feet in thickness, having a lining of firebrick, and a space or chamber for the admission of cold air between the exterior and interior of the stack. The air is admitted through holes in the ground, which lead to apertures in the foundation of the stack; these holes are covered with gratings. Nearly 300,000 bricks have been employed in this erection. This huge chimney is on a bank about 25 or 30 feet above the ground where the furnaces are built, and a flue or culvert slopes upwards from the culvert behind the furnaces to the base of the chimney, which is 150 feet from the culvert connected with the furnaces.

The Assay Office in connection with this establishment is very complete, and fitted up with every convenience; the draughts necessary for blowing the fires are introduced from the large culvert near the great chimney. There are two or three furnaces of different descriptions, and a sand bath for boiling chemical tests in porcelain vessels; to prevent any danger from the fumes, there is a glass cover over the sand bath, so that the operator can watch the process, while the fumes are carried through a flue to the outside of the building. Mr. Ludwig Seeger, of the University of Munich, has the appointment of Assayer and Analytical Chemist, and rejoices in the completeness of the establishment over which he presides.

There are also four large furnaces for burning the yellow sulphuret Ores, to drive off the sulphur, before putting them into the smelting furnaces. A few bushels of wood are sufficient to start them, and the Ore will continue to burn fiercely until the sulphur is consumed; a great saving of fuel is thus effected. There is a crushing engine of 16-horse power, for reducing the Ore to powder before smelting. The offices, &c., in connection with the establishment, make it as complete as could be desired.

The erection of these immense works was planned and designed by Messrs. G. & E. Hamilton, Architects and Civil Engineers, Adelaide, and I believe they received several suggestions, as to the practical part, from Mr. Lysson Jones, the Superintendent of the smelting, and formerly of the Patent Copper Company's Works at the Burra, and more recently of Kapunda.

About 150 hands are employed here, besides wood-carters, and the rate at which pure Copper is made is, at present, from 36 to 40 tons per week; but much more could be accomplished if the works were in full operation.

The Burra and Port Smelting Works

WERE commenced in the year 1849, at the Burra, by the Patent Copper Company, under the management of G. S. Walters, Esq., and Mr. Williams, the former at the Adelaide office, and the latter at the works. The present Manager of the Company is James Hamilton, Esq. The process of smelting is that known as Napier's Patent. The works at Port Adelaide have been erected by the present Company ("The English and Australian Copper Company") for the double purpose of extending the sphere of their operations, and of managing the smelting of the Burra Ores more economically, by balancing the cartage of Ore to the Port Works, with that of coal to the Burra, so that the waggons never travel empty.

Fourteen years since the Patent Copper Company entered into a contract for seven years with the Burra Company to purchase all the Ores from the Mine on certain conditions; paying according to the produce of pure Copper obtained from the Ore; and at the termination of that contract it was renewed, or a fresh contract made, for another term of seven years, which period has nearly expired. This Company has done much in the way of repairing the roads used by their teams, and has built bridges over several creeks. Some years ago they imported a large number of mules direct from Chili, with drivers to manage them; and hundreds of these animals, besides horses, are constantly employed in carting. In the former almost impassable state of the roads, the mules were sometimes made to carry the Ore in packs to Port Wakefield, whence it was shipped in barges to Port Adelaide. The arrangements of the Company appear to be very complete, and, did time permit, a history of their operations in the colony would be interesting; but I must content myself with little more than a brief description of their smelting establishments at the Burra and Port Adelaide.

At the time of my visit hands were scarce, both at the Mine and the Smelting Works; and of the 14 furnaces only 5 were at work, turning out about 120 tons of pure Copper per month, or

£10,800 worth. On some occasions more than this has has been done in a week. In one year the Company made the immense quantity of 3,087 tons of pure Copper from Burra Ores, and at the Works near the Mine the value of the Copper being about £290,000; 135 tons have been made in one week. There are 11 ordinary furnaces and three refineries, and fine Copper is made from carbonate Ores in only two operations, the fluxes used being iron and limestone. Each charge is from two tons to two and a quarter tons in weight. Fire bricks of excellent quality are made on the spot from fire clay procured about 12 miles distant ; a cupola kiln being employed for burning the bricks, and which holds 27,000 at once. These bricks stand better than the best Dinas, Stourbridge, or other imported bricks. Splendid fire clay is now obtained in many parts of the colony, and fire bricks made near some of the principal Mines. The stables contain stalls for 30 horses, besides loose boxes for half a dozen more ; there are also commodious yards and paddocks for the mules, and every appliance and convenience necessary for repairing the waggons, and shoeing the animals. The offices are convenient, and, besides clerks', accountants', and Captain Killicoat's (Manager) offices, comprise an assay office well-fitted up. Laborers' wages are from 35s. to 40s. per week ; smelters' from 58s. 6d. to 77s ; helpers from 45s. to 69s. The higher amounts may, in some cases, include overtime.

It is unnecessary to add any description of the Smelting Works at Port Adelaide ; suffice it to say that they comprise seven furnaces and one refinery, and the foundations of eight more are nearly completed. The number of handse mployed at the two establishments, independent of carters, varies from about 120 to 250, according to the amount of work in hand.

From the above account it will be seen that the works of the English and Australian Copper Company have been productive of great benefit to the colony from the large amount of capital expended here, and the hundreds of hands employed in various ways. During last year they expended £7,000, for feed for horses and mules. I believe the Company are anxious to extend their operations by making arrangements with Mine proprietors for the purchase of Ore on terms as good, or better, than they could realize by shipping it to England.

Mr. Rodda's Process.

I PROCEED now to describe a new process of reducing Ores, invented and patented in this colony by the late Captain R. V. Rodda, of Angaston. The peculiarity of this process consists in the fusion of the metallic particles alone, while the stony portions of the Ore retain their original form, though deprived of much of their weight, and of certain other qualities ; and this enables them to be more easily crushed, while the metallized part is more readily separated. A great saving in fuel is thus effected, the heat required for this process being only about 2,000 °, Far.; while to smelt Ores, by the old method, nearly double that heat is necessary. No flux is required, and the expense is ascertained to be only £1 per ton on Ores containing no sulphur. Thus poor Ores can be dealt with which are now rejected as worthless. A great saving in time is also effected ; three charges, equal to three tons, have been treated in 15 hours, less than two tons of wood and only one cwt. of coal being consumed. Other Ores can also be dealt with—Iron Ores being easily formed into wrought Iron without the usual process of first casting the metal.

This process has only been fairly put to the test at the New Cornwall Mines, and I will give Mr. Rodda's (Captain R's. son) own description of the furnaces there :—

"The present furnace at the New Cornwall Mines is constructed with three soles or floors ; on the top floor, which is in fact the roof of the furnace below it, the Ores are first placed to be dried and heated by the surplus heat of the fire underneath. The hot Ore broken to about half inch guage, and mixed with about an equal quantity of charcoal, is then let down on to the middle floor, when it is raised to a dull red heat. Communication with the outer air is then shut off, and the combustion of the charcoal is only sustained by the oxygen contained in the Ores themselves. In parting with its oxygen the metallic portion of the Ore is converted from its friable and compound state into a simple and metallic condition, and at this stage of the process the charge is let down into the lowest furnace, when the heat is increased till the metal is thoroughly fused, the particles of the metal being found to run together into granules under the influence of molecular attraction. The furnace process is then completed ; the charge is drawn, the unconsumed charcoal is separated from the Ore by flotation in water, and the granules and metal from the stone by crushing and washing. The crushing and washing are estimated to cost about 5s. per ton with proper machinery, and even with the rude appliances hitherto available for this purpose the Copper left in the tailings, after washing, is found to amount to less than one quarter per cent."

This discovery is likely to prove of great benefit to the colony, and a Company has been formed to carry out the working of the plan.

Mineral Regulations.

I ALLUDED briefly to our Mineral Regulations, as they are called, in the introductory chapter, but I propose now to consider the subject more in detail. The Act of Parliament passed last session—No. 24 of 1862—and assented to by the Governor-in-Chief in the name and on behalf of the Queen, on the 21st October, 1862, may be thus briefly summarized :—Leases of the Waste Lands of the Crown may be granted by the Governor, for the purpose of mining for any mineral except Gold, the quantity of land leased in any one block to be not more than 320 acres, and the term of the lease not to exceed 14 years. The rent payable to the Government is fixed at 10s per acre; and the right of renewing the lease at the end of the term is secured to the lessee for two further periods of 14 years on payment of what is called a *fine* on each renewal; the fine to be not less than £1 nor more than £20 per acre. After paying the first year's rent the lessee has right of search for one year, before taking out his lease, thus gaining actually a term of 15 years before having to pay the fine for renewal. No Ore, however (except one ton for samples, I believe), must be removed before the lease is agreed. The rent is payable yearly in advance, and the lessee is required to spend in labor, on the ground, £6 per acre, during every two years, or to employ three men for at least nine months in each year. The lessee may determine the lease by giving three months' notice of his intention; but should he desire to renew the lease he must give notice twelve months before the expiry of the first lease; and the Government will fix the amount of the fine three months before the lease expires.

These are the principal regulations respecting the leasing and working of mineral lands in South Australia, and they are regarded as far from satisfactory by those persons engaged in mining pursuits.

There is some little improvement on the old regulations, but still anyone conversant with mining will see that very little encouragement is afforded to persons desirous of developing the mineral wealth of the country. The clause compelling the lessee to expend £6 per acre on the ground every two years, was no doubt introduced to prevent anything like a dog-in-the-manger action on the part of holders of mineral lands, and so far it may be all very well; but it may also operate very prejudicially in another direction There are also certain practical difficulties thrown in the way, so that if some slight error be made in describing the position of a claim, or in surveying it, the original discoverer may be deprived of his just right, by some interloper who is more fortunate in the surveyor he employs, or in his own powers of description, or organ of " locality."

These things are managed better in Cornwall, and though we are apt sometimes to laugh at " Cousin Jack" we might occasionally gain some useful lessons from him. In the Duchy of

Cornwall persons can search for metal anywhere, on land not previously claimed, without being called upon to pay 10s. an acre on a described claim, for the *right of search ;* they may peg out a claim without fear of being molested, unless another comes to search alongside of them, when they may be called on to define their boundaries ; and as the payment is made in the shape of a Royalty on the Ore raised, they don't have to *pay for nothing,* as is too often the case with us. In Cornwall, if a man wishes to shift the pegs marking his boundary he can do so provided he interferes with no one else, without having to incur the expense of a survey ; here, if he discover that his claim is a little too much one way or the other, he must go to the expense of a new survey, which will cost £15 or £20, and after all he may get no Ore in paying quantities. Moreover, the surveys may be disputed, as the bearings of the Government trigs are sometimes said, by the surveyors, to be incorrect. It is palpable that there should be some difference made between the rent paid on claims producing nothing and on those which yield 500 tons of Ore, or more, per month. There are two plans open to the Government, either of which, I believe, would be more popular and generally satisfactory than those now in operation. The first is a Royalty, but that has its objections, and was strongly opposed when hinted at some years since ; the better plan wou'd perhaps be an export duty on all Ores or Metals, this would be more easily collected than a Royalty, and in many respects preferable—witness how well the export duty on Gold has worked in Victoria.

I have not time to enlarge on this subject, but have thrown out a few rough hints, which, if duly considered and acted upon by our legislators, may tend to bring about an improved state of things in respect to our Mineral Regulations, and, instead of our energies being crippled, there will be every incentive to vigorous exertion.

I now proceed to refer to the proposed

Railway to the Northern Mines.

THIS is usually but incorrectly spoken of as a tramway. A tramway, strictly speaking, is a line of wooden rails plated with iron whereas I belive it has never been contemplated to lay down, from Port Augusta northwards anything but regular iron rails, though of a lighter weight than those used where great speed and heavy carriage are required. The weight of rail suggested by Mr. Hamilton, and adopted by Parliament, is 35 lbs. to the yard, and the speed required eight miles per hour, including stoppages. Mr. George Ernest Hamilton, C.E., made an inspection of the proposed route, at the request of Mr. Bonney, the Manager in Adelaide of the Great Northern Mining Company, and his report, which is a very favorable one, was laid before Parliament and printed by order of the House. The report, though interesting,

is too lengthy for insertion here; but I shall condense the sub-
stance of it:—The country is unusually favorable for the construction of a railway for at least 100 miles from Port Augusta,
along the Western Plain. [The route is marked on the map
accompanying this book.] It might, if expedient, be then extended through the Parachilna Gap to the neighbourhood of
Patawarta. This would bring it very near to the Nuccaleena
and Blinman Mines, and into a rich, but at present to a great
extent undeveloped, mineral country. It might also, if advisable,
be extended northwards along the Plain past Mount Deception,
Mount Coffin, and Mount Lyndhurst, where we know there is a
valuable Mine; and then a very large tract of pastoral country
would be benefitted by the facilities offered for the carriage of
wool. The idea of the extension to Mount Lyndhurst is my own,
and I believe I am correct in saying that there are scarcely any
engineering difficulties in the way. I am not, however, prepared
to say whether that route would be warranted by the immediate
prospects of traffic; but, as I believe the Western Plains a few
miles north of Mount Lyndhurst are only about 15 miles from
the Yudanamutana, and the Sir Dominick, Daly, Stanley, and other
Mines, and also not far from the Mount Rose (a very rich Mine)
further South, it would be worth consideration whether, with the
prospect of a large supply of Ore from this district, and the probability of a quantity of wool from the North and North-west, a
continuation of the line would not be advisable. Since writing
the above I have been favored with the sight of a supplementary
report by Mr. G. E. Hamilton, written at the close of last year,
and in which he alludes to the route I have suggested as being
less expensive of construction, though of greater length to the
Mines, than that through the hills by Patawarta; and he says if
the general opening up of the country is considered, without
special reference to the Mines, the route along the Western
Plains might be the most desirable, as it is the most practicable.
Still it must be considered that the bulk of the traffic would come
from the Mines; and it is just a question of expense, taking all
things into account, whether a railway along the Plains, within
15 miles of several Mines, or direct to the Mines through the
hills, would be the best. Mr. Hamilton estimates the distance
from Port Augusta to, the Yudanamutana Mines, by way of
Burr's Creek (through the hills) at 230 miles; by the present
road it is at least 20 miles more. Mr. Hamilton in his first
report, dated August 1860, estimates that the stores, wool, and
other produce for and from 10,000 square miles of country would
be forwarded by this railway; and would yield a return, independent of the Mines, to the amount of £15,000 a year. I consider
this a fair and moderate estimate, and would add that a great
deal more country has been taken up since then, that the
squatters are sending more sheep up in place of cattle, and that
some really valuable mineral discoveries have been made in the
North since 1860. The Yudanamutana Company, alone, could
better afford to pay £30,000 a year cartage to the railway (for

10,000 tons of Ore at £3 a ton), than they can now afford to pay drays for 3,000 tons at an average of £7 per ton; and their Mines must be very inferior to what I believe them to be, if they cannot from all raise 10,000 tons of Ore per annum. If this be the case the railway could, without doubt, as Mr. Hamilton believes, pay the promoters six per cent. on the outlay; and, I believe, they would have at least three or four per cent. for a reserve or sinking fund. Then it must be remembered that there are other Mines, as yet undeveloped, but likely to prove exceedingly rich, and which would add largely to the traffic, if the formation of a railway induced the working of them.

Without a railway I am convinced that nine-tenths of the Northern Mines must be practically worthless; but with this important auxilliary to their successful working, wealth almost unimagined may be developed, and employment found for thousands of persons. Even the Yudanamutana Mines cannot be expected long to be able to pay the high rate of cartage at present ruling; for Ores of less than 35 or 40 per cent. from that distant locality do not leave a reasonable profit.

By an Act (No. 28, of 1862), passed at the close of last session, our Parliament have agreed to make a grant of the land required for the construction of the railway, for a breadth of two chains along the line, and a grant of blocks of land in contiguity with the line, equal to two square miles for every mile of length, and which may be selected by the promoters, on either side of the line; but not more than 20 square miles in one block, and the shape to be a parallelogram, half as wide as it is long. These liberal terms, with the prospects of success, surely ought to be sufficient to induce capitalists to undertake the work.

I think I have already stated the population of the country North of Port Augusta to be above 6,000, and the following return of letters received at Kanyaka, and despatched therefrom, during the year 1862, may not be out of place as an evidence of the importance of the Northern districts. Letters received 23,305, despatched 21,598. I am indebted for this information to the Postmaster-General. There is now a weekly mail to and from Yudanamutana, embracing all the intermediate stations.

Conclusion.

I HAVE now completed my labors, and I can conscientiously say that I have given a true and faithful account of our Mines, to the best of my judgment, and from a personal inspection of nearly all of them. Respecting some there may be a difference of opinion; but this there often is between professional men who have for many years been practically engaged in Mining; indeed, I have been astonished to hear the diametrically opposite opinions sometimes expressed by men of equal knowledge and experience. I have had no inducement to speak favorably of any Mine, or unfavorably; my object, in writing this book, has been to give correct information for the benefit of the public, and especially for the good of the colony; for I believe, when the immensity of our mineral resources is known, benefit must result to the country.

Nearly every known mineral has at some time or other been found here, although at present those which are known to exist, in any considerable quantities, are only Iron, Copper, Lead, Silver (in Galena), Bismuth, Manganese, Zinc, Plumbago, and Gold (the last in not very large quantities comparatively speaking). Of these Manganese and Zinc exist in combination with other Ores, and are not made any use of.

The discovery of Bismuth, on the Stanley Mine, the property of the Northern Mineral Association, is likely to prove of some importance; and I am informed that a promising Mine of Plumbago is being worked, or about to be so, in the neighbourhood of Port Lincoln.

In reading over the proof sheets it occurs to me that I might have spoken rather more favorably than I have of the Apex Hill Mine; and also of the Wheal Austin.

I have been requested by several persons interested in mining to make some allusion to the high rate of wages current at the present time. I have given quotations in various parts of the book, and may state generally that the lowest rate of laborers' wages is 4s. 6d. per day, while some earn as much as 7s. 6d. Miners' wages vary from 5s. 6d. to 9s. 6d. per day, the latter rate being paid on the more remote Mines, and to the best men; boys from 2s. to 3s. 6d. Tributers have the chance of making more or less according to their "luck." Refiners on some of the smelting works earn 12s. per day, and masons the same; carters and stablemen, 5s. 10d. to 6s. 8d. per day. In speaking of the rate of wages I should also name the price of flour and meat. The price of the former is one penny farthing to three half pence per lb., and of the latter from 2d. to 6d. per lb. Far be it from me to wish to grind down the laborer, who is worthy of his hire, if he does a fair day's work; but I think when compared with the rates paid in England it will be seen that miners are better off in this country. The complaints of employers are unanimous as to the difficulty of working Mines here on account of the rate of wages. I have sometimes been witness to the independent spirit of some men, who seem the more discontented the higher their wages, and who have not the slightest compunction in causing their employers great inconvenience by suddenly leaving them, even at a critical time; and I have often known of men earning enough to keep them well, by working three days a week, and idling the rest of their time. I believe the conscientious, industrious, and provident miner or laborer will find that in this country he will be secure of a fair day's wages for a fair fair day's work, and will have far better opportunity of settling his family well here than in the old country.

The last mail from the North, (19th March), brings highly favourable accounts from the Yudanamutana Mine, and mentions fine lodes being cut in two parts of the property recently opened.

The West Kanmantoo Mine is also shewing very satisfactory results, and the shares in the New Company are, I believe, nearly all taken up. Nearly 50 tons of splended black sulphuret Ore are now raised from the lode which I saw opened, at 8 fathoms, not 10 as stated—besides nearly an equal quantity of Ore of less produce.

The Talisker Silver Lead Mine continues to improve, and its stability and richness may now be considered as fully established. Since writing my notice of this Mine, returns have been received from England of an assay made by the Messrs. Johnson of one ton of the Ore, which yielded 60 per cent. of fine Lead, and $62\frac{1}{4}$ ozs. of Silver to the ton of Ore. The estimate I gave of 30 to 40 ozs. of Silver was, doubtless, within the mark as an average of the whole produce of the Mine.

The lode in the Kurilla Mine has improved considerably during the past week, and some rich yellow Ore has been raised; the lode is said now to be yielding from 3 to 4 tons per fathom.

A fine discovery of Silver-lead Ore is just reported as having been made on the property of Mr. P. B. Coglin, M.P., between Rapid Bay and Cape Jervis. I have seen samples of the Ore, which is really splendid, a piece from just below the surface having yielded, on assay, 80 per cent. of Lead and 12 ounces of Silver to the ton of Ore. The lode is traceable through two sections, or for a length of about a mile.

The Bremer and other standard Mines are also progressing very satisfactorily. The Karkarilla Mine also is said, by a telegram received on 20th March, to be "looking better than ever, the lode, 18 inches wide, and very good." The Captainis report of same date, since received, says they are raising some good Ore.

Other discoveries are reported almost daily, but I have heard of nothing of special importance; and if I were to continue to write about all the mineral discoveries as they are announced I should never have done.

I have mentioned these in order to give the latest information possible.

In conclusion, I have to apologise for some typographical errors, the principal of which will be found corrected below, and also for the roughness of the map, which was copied from one hastily drawn by myself. It is, however, tolerably correct, quite sufficiently so for the purpose for which it was intended; although I regret to say there are one or two slight inaccuracies in the relative positions of some of the Mines on Yorke's Peninsula.

It was almost impossible in a lithographed map, drawn on so small a scale, to mark down every mineral claim, but all the principal Mines are named, and the mark inserted in other places to shew the existence of mineral. The lithographers have committed a slight error in saying " Townships, &c., marked ▓."

Many of the places so marked being merely sheep or cattle stations ; most of the townships and few stations are south of the Burra, while all to the north of Kooringa, except Melrose and Kanyaka, are stations.

I am sensible of the defects of this little work, which has been written under circumstances of some difficulty, but I trust they will be viewed leniently, and that the object of the book will be answered.

ERRATA.—Page 40, line 16, for " grey," read "green." Page 41, line 11, for " 300," read " 260 " Page 53, Pindilpena Mine, line 8, for "88," read " 80 " There may be other trifling errors, but the above are all which I have observed worth correcting.

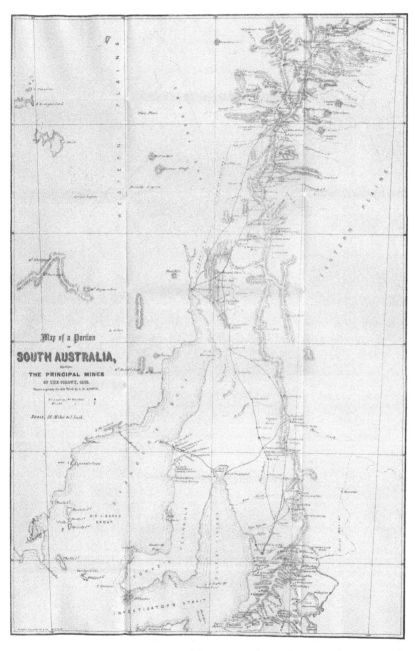

The material originally positioned here is too large for reproduction in this reissue. A PDF can be downloaded from the web address given on page iv of this book, by clicking on 'Resources Available'.